Judgment as Structure

Judgment as Structure

On Responsibility, Structure, and Legitimate Judgment

Xiaoqing Wang

This volume provides no directives.

Copyright © 2026 Xiaoqing Wang

All rights reserved.

No part of this book may be reproduced, stored in a retrieval system, or transmitted in any form or by any means—electronic, mechanical, photocopying, recording, or otherwise— without prior written permission of the publisher, except for brief quotations in reviews.

This book is a work of nonfiction. It does not provide advice, instruction, or guidance of any kind.

ISBN: 979-8-9947559-1-4

Contents

1 The Effort That Didn't Matter   1

2 Effort Without Response Is Not a Personal Failure 24

3 When effort becomes a trap   57

4 How judgment illusions are constructed   86

5 Feedback Loops That Never Close   121

6 Why systems quietly reward over-responsibility   153

7 What judgment authority is not   182

8 How the absence of authority disguises itself   214

9 Recognition without resolution   243

10 Why action does not follow 271

11 The necessary blank 306

Structural Preface

This volume does not teach judgment.

It defines the structural conditions under which judgment can exist, remain valid, or fail. The text that follows is not organized to guide a reader, but to formalize a system.

Judgment is treated here as a structural phenomenon rather than a personal capacity. It is not evaluated by outcomes, persuasion, or authority, but by whether its internal conditions are satisfied. When those conditions are absent, judgment collapses regardless of intent, intelligence, or experience.

This book therefore makes no promises to the reader. It offers no methods, no prescriptions, and no guidance for action. Its purpose is to describe a framework within which judgment may be recognized, examined, and invalidated.

The chapters are arranged as structural components rather than a learning sequence. They may be read non-linearly. No chapter assumes agreement with the author, nor requires acceptance of prior claims beyond the definitions stated within the system itself.

Where examples appear, they function as boundary illustrations, not as instruction. Where assertions are made, they describe constraints, not advice. Silence is preferred to explanation where explanation would introduce interpretation.

This volume stands independently of application. Subsequent works may refer to this structure, rely on it, or instantiate it in specific contexts, but they do not extend or modify it. The structure defined here is intentionally closed.

If judgment is present, it must be present within these constraints. If it is absent, no external authority can supply it.

This document exists to make that distinction explicit.

Chapter 1

The Effort That Didn't Matter

Most people do not consciously choose to carry outcomes that are not theirs.

They inherit them.

Not through instruction, but through repetition. Not through agreement, but through exposure.

From an early age, you are taught to associate effort with result, intention with outcome, responsibility with control. These associations are not presented as theories. They are embedded in everyday language. "You should have known." "You could have done more." "If you cared enough, this wouldn't have happened." The wording is simple, but the message is strong: if an outcome is bad, there must have been a better version of you who could have prevented it.

Over time, these statements stop sounding like accusations. They begin to feel like descriptions of reality. And once that happens, something subtle but permanent takes place: you begin to experience outcomes as if they were evidence of your internal state. Success feels like proof of worth. Failure feels like proof of deficiency. Ambiguous results feel like unresolved guilt. It becomes natural to look at what happened and immediately search for what it says about you.

None of this requires anyone to explicitly tell you, "You are responsible for everything that happens." The structure teaches it for them. You watch adults defend outcomes that were never fully in their control. You hear them apologize for delays that were caused by systems, weather, timing, or other people's decisions. You see them interpret a good result as a reflection of character and a bad result as a reflection of negligence. You do not need a formal lesson when the environment already has a rhythm.

So you learn a kind of emotional arithmetic. Effort is treated as a deposit. Outcomes are treated as returns. When the return is missing, you assume the deposit was insufficient. If the return is unexpected, you assume the deposit must have been larger than you realized. The world begins to feel like a ledger, and your sense of self becomes the balance.

That ledger becomes the default way of reading experience. A good day feels like a reward earned. A bad day feels like a penalty deserved. Neutral days feel like missed opportunities to prove that you are doing enough. You are not told to read days this way, but you absorb the reading because everyone around you seems to do it. The calibration is cultural before it becomes personal.

This is how outcome-carrying becomes normal. It begins with language, is reinforced by observation, and settles into the background as common sense. It does not feel like a belief. It feels like a reality. And reality is rarely interrogated.

Part of the inheritance is a cultural story about merit. In that story, results reveal character. The story is appealing because it simplifies the world. If outcomes are earned, then the world is legible. If outcomes are controlled, then effort is safe. A person can survive uncertainty by believing that the right choices will be rewarded. The belief is not entirely false, but it is incomplete, and the mind treats incompletion as irrelevant.

This story is repeated in biographies, interviews, and everyday retellings. Success is presented as the product of perseverance, failure as the product of inadequate resolve. The role of timing, access, and chance is minimized, not always out of dishonesty, but because the story needs a protagonist. The protagonist is the self, so the story emphasizes the self. A person absorbs this rhythm and begins to hear their own outcomes as personal narratives, even when the plot includes forces they did not choose.

There is also a social function to the story. If outcomes are personal, then praise and blame have a clear destination. People can reward a person without studying the system. They can assign fault without untangling complexity. Praise and blame are efficient. Efficiency makes them attractive, and repetition makes them feel accurate. The individual becomes the container for what the system cannot easily explain.

Pride and shame both rely on the same structure. They attach emotion to results and then attach results to the self. A good outcome becomes a reason to feel worthy. A bad outcome becomes a reason to feel defective. The emotions differ, but the logic is identical. The more a person participates in that logic, the more difficult it becomes to notice that the logic itself is optional.

The mind prefers a story with a single author. A system is diffuse and difficult to hold. A person is concrete and familiar. When ambiguity appears, the mind gravitates toward the personal because it is easier to imagine. The personal story is vivid, the systemic story is abstract. Even when you can intellectually describe the system, the emotional weight lands on the person because the person is where the emotion lives.

Comparison reinforces this. You see someone else with a different outcome and you assume a difference in internal qualities. You rarely see the invisible variables that shaped their result. You see their outcome and your outcome, and the gap becomes a statement about you. The more you compare, the more you internalize the outcome as a personal verdict.

When a result diverges from your hopes, the moral story demands an explanation. The mind provides one by narrowing the cause to the self. This restores order, even if it is painful. The pain feels honest because it creates a sense of fairness. In this way, self-blame can feel like integrity. It is not chosen; it is absorbed as part of the story of how the world works.

There is a quiet assumption operating beneath most modern lives:

If something matters to you, you are responsible for how it turns out.

At first glance, this sounds reasonable. Even ethical. It flatters agency and seems to honor care. It allows people to feel that attention has power, that the world responds to their effort. It aligns with a familiar moral story: if you try hard and you are good, things should work. The assumption feels like a virtue and a comfort at the same time.

It is also reinforced by the moments when it appears true. Sometimes effort does correlate with outcome. Sometimes intention does lead to a better result. In those moments, the assumption feels validated, and the mind treats the validation as proof. The fact that it was one of many variables does not register; the person was present, the effort was felt, the result arrived. The story locks in.

But notice how quickly it collapses under pressure. Outcomes are not single-variable systems. They are intersections of timing, incentives, constraints, other people's actions, randomness, and structural limits—most of which are invisible to the individual inside the situation. Your effort can be one factor among many, and sometimes it is not even a decisive factor. Yet when the result arrives, the mind searches for a single point of attribution. The closest, most emotionally available candidate is always the self.

This is not because the self caused the outcome. It is because the self is present when the outcome is revealed. Presence is mistaken for authorship. Being there when the result appears creates the illusion that you must have been responsible for what it is. The mind reaches for a handle, and the self is the handle that is always in reach.

The environment often cooperates with this illusion. Outcomes are delivered in ways that emphasize the individual. Performance reviews, grades, rankings, feedback forms, social reactions—these are all designed to point toward a person. The system needs a place to put the result, and the person is the most accessible place. The complexity of the system is not addressed because the system must move on.

So the person absorbs the weight. This absorption feels like maturity. It looks like accountability. It is praised as ownership. But there is a difference between accountability and authorship. Accountability is a social role; authorship is a causal claim. The mind often treats them as the same, because they are presented together.

When you are the person connected to the outcome, you are expected to speak for it. You are asked to explain it, to justify it, to defend it. Over time, you begin to feel that if you must speak for it, you must have caused it. The act of explanation becomes an act of self-assignment.

This misattribution does not merely create discomfort. It reshapes behavior. People begin to optimize not for clarity, but for control. They overextend, over-explain, over-own. They treat uncertain outcomes as if they were personal obligations. They apologize for delays caused by systems. They internalize market responses. They personalize institutional failures. They feel compelled to justify themselves to a world that was never asking for justification, because they have already decided that the outcome is a reflection of their adequacy.

The need to justify becomes a constant background task. You anticipate questions that may never come. You create explanations for outcomes that were not actually up to you. The explanation is not only for others; it is also for yourself. If you can explain the outcome, you can feel as though you had a place in shaping it. The explanation turns complexity into a story that can be held, even if the story assigns the weight to you.

This can look like professionalism. It can look like integrity. A person who takes responsibility seems trustworthy, and so the behavior is reinforced. The reinforcement does not discriminate between what was within control and what was not. The praise is for the posture, not the causal reality. Over time, the posture becomes identity, and the identity makes it harder to notice when the outcome is being carried unnecessarily.

And perhaps most dangerously, they learn to preempt blame by assuming it in advance. "I should have anticipated this." "I should have prevented that." "I should have been better." Notice the grammar. These statements are framed as reflections, but they function as retroactive contracts: agreements signed after the fact, binding the individual to outcomes they never had authority over. The sentence sounds like humility, but it creates a permanent claim against the self.

This pattern is difficult to notice because it often coincides with competence. Highly capable people are especially vulnerable to this distortion. Because they can influence outcomes sometimes, they are gradually trained to believe they should influence them always. The boundary between influence and authority erodes, not through failure, but through partial success. Each time effort correlates with improvement, the mind draws a stronger line than reality supports.

When the correlation breaks—as it inevitably does—the mind does not revise the model. It revises the self. The conclusion is not "this system is complex." The conclusion is "I must have missed something." Competence becomes a trap because it offers evidence of control without revealing its limits. It rewards the assumption until the assumption is no longer survivable.

Even the language of improvement can intensify this. When people say "learn from it" or "do better next time," they are often offering care. But the listener can hear these phrases as confirmation that the outcome was theirs to own. The subtle implication is that a correct adjustment would have prevented the result. The mind absorbs that implication even if no one intended it.

In professional life, this pattern is often invisible because it looks like dedication. A project runs behind because a vendor misses a deadline, a policy changes, or a market shifts. The team hits a wall that was never visible at the start. Even when everyone can name the external causes, someone still feels personally responsible. The person closest to the work hears the outcome as commentary on their ability. The mind tightens around the result, not because the person is reckless, but because they were present.

The closer you are to the outcome, the more the outcome feels like a statement about you. If you were the one who made the plan, then a deviation feels like an exposure. If you were the one who communicated expectations, then the failure of those expectations feels like your error. If you were the one who cared most, then the disappointment seems to belong to you. The reality of shared causation does not dissolve the internal claim.

The phrase "take ownership" appears in many workplaces as a compliment. It implies initiative and responsibility. But it also blurs lines. Ownership suggests control, and control suggests authorship. A person can do everything asked and still carry the emotional weight of an outcome that was never theirs to determine. They become the face of a system, and the system's volatility becomes a reflection on their steadiness.

When numbers are involved, the effect intensifies. Revenue, adoption, retention, ratings, satisfaction scores—these are outcomes with many drivers, yet they are often attached to a single role. The person in that role can feel as if their judgment is on trial every time the numbers update. A slight dip becomes a personal failure, even if the causes were external. A strong result brings relief rather than security, because it confirms that the stakes were personal.

The same happens in fields where the outcome is a deliverable. A launch is delayed, a client changes direction, a legal review introduces a new constraint. The outcome moves, and the person responsible for the timeline feels the movement as a reflection on their competence. The frustration is real. The ownership becomes internal. The person feels that they should have anticipated the unanticipated.

In education, outcomes arrive with symbols that feel definitive: grades, rankings, scores, acceptance letters. These are clean signals in messy environments. The effort that went into learning is not measured; the outcome is. You can do the work and still receive a result that does not reflect the work, and yet the mind still converts the outcome into a statement about ability. The system does not need to speak. The silence is enough to make the result feel personal.

The group project intensifies this. The shared outcome does not make shared responsibility feel lighter. It makes each person feel exposed. If someone else fails to do their part, you can still feel it as your failure. If the group succeeds, you may feel relief rather than credit. The outcome lands on the self even when the control was distributed. You feel you should have managed the distribution, as if the ability to control others was part of the assignment.

Even the most ordinary classroom feedback can have this effect. A teacher says, "You can do better," and it lands not as encouragement but as evidence that the current result is a personal failure. The intention might be care, but the internal translation becomes ownership of the outcome. It becomes another data point in the ledger.

Competitive environments amplify this because scarcity is built into the structure. There are limited seats, limited roles, limited prizes. When someone else receives the slot, you can feel as though you were personally rejected, even if the decision was a reflection of timing, fit, or a small difference in an evaluator's preference. Scarcity turns outcomes into judgments. The system does not need to say you were inadequate; the result feels like the statement.

Family roles form another early template. Many people are implicitly assigned a role as the steady one, the mediator, the responsible child. That role can begin as a compliment and end as a duty. When conflict arises, the responsible one feels accountable for resolution. When a parent is unhappy, the responsible one looks inward. The outcome of other people's emotional lives becomes a private burden. The family may never say it aloud, but the role still shapes the internal sense of responsibility.

Team settings can extend this role into adulthood. Dependencies are distributed, but accountability is often centralized. You may be the person who communicates with the client or the person who coordinates the timeline, and so the outcome feels like yours even when another part of the system failed. You become the translator of uncertainty, the buffer between chaos and expectation. That buffering can be praised, but it also assigns the outcome to you.

Service roles add another layer because you represent a system that you cannot change. A customer is angry at a policy, a patient is distressed by a wait, a guest is disappointed by a constraint. You are the visible surface, so the outcome is directed at you. Even when you know the system is at fault, the emotional impact can still feel personal. The responsibility is felt because the interaction is personal.

Creative work carries its own version of outcome ownership. The reception of a piece of work is unpredictable, filtered through taste, timing, and context. Yet the response is often felt as a direct reflection of the self. Praise feels like a momentary relief, criticism feels like a statement about identity. The outcome is not only professional; it is personal, because the work came from you.

Legal, bureaucratic, and regulatory outcomes can be just as heavy. A visa is delayed, a permit is denied, a decision is postponed. You have followed the steps, yet the outcome still does not arrive. The system is opaque, but the delay feels like a personal failure. The mind assumes that if the outcome is negative, it must be because something was not done correctly, even when the system provides no clear cause.

In relationships, the boundary between care and control dissolves easily. Someone you love is unhappy. A conversation goes badly. A long-term plan changes shape. The emotional impulse is to absorb the outcome as proof that you did not love enough, listen enough, anticipate enough. Even when another person's response is clearly rooted in their own history, the mind treats it as a verdict on your adequacy. There is no scoreboard, yet you feel scored.

The same pattern appears in conflict. If someone is upset, you scan your memory for the moment when you could have prevented it. The mind does this automatically. It searches for the earlier decision that would have altered the outcome. When it finds a possible point, even if it is hypothetical, it becomes evidence of responsibility. You end up carrying not only what happened, but every imagined alternative that might have been better.

In caregiving, the pattern becomes sharper. A parent, a partner, a friend, or a colleague is in pain. Their experience cannot be engineered into a better outcome, but the desire to help makes it feel as if it should be. When pain persists, the caregiver feels like the cause. The gap between care and control is interpreted as a moral gap. That interpretation is silent, so it feels true.

The caregiver hears their own limitations as failure. A person can do everything available and still watch someone suffer. The suffering becomes a reflection on them, because love was involved. The more they care, the more personal the outcome feels. There is no external accusation, but there is an internal sense of responsibility that is hard to shake.

Physical health creates a similar burden. You can follow every instruction, be disciplined, and still face outcomes that are not yours: a diagnosis that arrives without warning, a recovery that stalls, a body that does not respond to your efforts in the way you were told it should. The result feels like a personal failure even when it is clearly biological variance. The mind still converts the outcome into a story about what you did or did not do.

Even when the logic is clear, the emotion remains. "I did everything right" is a common sentence after a difficult outcome. The sentence is accurate, but it is also a confession of how much the outcome has been internalized. If the outcome were not felt as personal, the sentence would not be needed. It is a protest against an internal judge.

Financial life multiplies the problem because the signals are constant. You make a careful decision and the market moves in the opposite direction. You follow prudent guidance and an unexpected event undoes the plan. Even when you know the system is complex, the outcome can still feel like a verdict on judgment. The number on the statement looks definitive, and so it becomes personal.

The daily language of finance reinforces this. Words like "good decision" and "bad decision" are attached to results rather than process. If a market move was favorable, it was a good decision. If it was unfavorable, it was a bad one. The complexity disappears and the person is left with a simple label. The label sticks even when the person knows it should not.

Community and public life add another layer. Events unfold that are far larger than any individual. Policies shift. Institutions fail. A climate event alters a plan. Yet when you are embedded in the situation, you can still feel like the outcome is yours to carry. You are present, so the weight lands on you. The scale of the system does not protect you from the sense of personal responsibility; it often intensifies it, because there is nowhere else for the mind to place the weight.

In volunteer work, in community leadership, in mutual aid, people often take on outcomes precisely because they care. When something goes wrong, they feel as though they have failed a community, not just a task. The absence of formal authority does not reduce the sense of personal responsibility; it increases it, because the role is defined by care rather than control. The more you care, the more you carry.

Domestic life contains smaller versions of the same pattern. The house is a system with its own timing, its own glitches, its own tensions. A meal goes wrong, a plan falls apart, a calendar conflict breaks a promise. The outcome is often the product of several moving pieces, but it lands as personal failure because it was your attention that connected the pieces. The day becomes a chain of tiny outcomes, each one a quiet test of competence that you did not consciously agree to take.

The emotional climate of a household can also feel like a personal outcome. If the mood is tense, you look for the moment you created the tension. If someone else is quiet, you search for the thing you missed. This happens even when the other person's mood has nothing to do with you. The mind treats the atmosphere as an outcome and then asks who is responsible for it. You are nearby, so the responsibility falls inward.

Friendship and social life operate similarly. A message goes unanswered, a plan is canceled, a friend becomes distant. The rational explanation can be simple, but the emotional interpretation is personal. You replay the conversation to find the line you should not have said. You scan your calendar to see where you failed to show up. The outcome of someone else's silence becomes your own task to explain.

Gatherings make the pattern visible because they involve a group and yet feel like a personal test. If the energy is flat, you might feel as though you failed to create it. If people leave early, you might feel as though you did not hold their attention. The outcome is a collective product, but the mind seeks a single author. It often chooses the person who cared the most about how the evening would feel.

Public performance creates another variant. You present, audition, speak, or compete. The outcome depends on an audience, a judge, a timing, a room. Even when you know this, the result can feel like a verdict on your worth. The difference between a good day and a bad day becomes moral, even when it is simply situational. The evaluation lands inside because the evaluation is directed at you.

Digital and professional metrics sharpen the problem by providing constant signals. Views, likes, response times, ratings, and other forms of feedback appear to offer objective data. But they are still the results of systems with many variables. The mind tends to treat them as direct reflections of value. A number that fluctuates becomes a statement about you, even when the fluctuation reflects a platform change, an algorithm, or a shifting audience.

Administrative systems add their own weight. A form is submitted, a process stalls, a deadline moves. The system is slow or inconsistent, but the person involved feels responsible for the delay. There is a sense that if you had been more diligent, more precise, more attentive, the outcome would have been different. The system does not say this. The mind fills in the gap.

External silence and expectation drift make this heavier. When an outcome arrives, there is often no clear voice that says, "This was not yours." Silence is interpreted as confirmation. If people depend on your competence, they may not even realize they are letting you take on more than you have authority over. The absence of correction becomes a quiet permission.

Expectations also drift slowly. You handle something once, then you handle it again. The third time, it is no longer a favor. It is simply yours. No one announces that the boundary has shifted. No one signs a contract. The shift happens in the tone of an email, the assumption in a meeting, the absence of a question. You are carrying the outcome not because you were asked to, but because the pattern has settled.

This drift often feels like recognition. Being trusted can feel like being valued, and so the added weight is accepted without resistance. But the weight includes outcomes you cannot fully influence. A role expands while the authority does not. The responsibility is clear; the control is partial. Over time, the role becomes a container for other people's uncertainty, and you become the person who absorbs it.

Role boundaries are often created by urgency rather than design. In a crisis, someone steps forward. After the crisis, the step forward becomes a position. The role is not questioned because it was useful. The system keeps moving, and the role hardens into an expectation. The person who stepped forward is still present, so the expectation feels natural. What began as situational becomes permanent without ever being named.

Reliability invites more dependence. When you are the one who notices the loose thread, others stop looking for it. When you are the one who follows through, others stop expecting themselves to do so. The redistribution happens quietly. It does not require anyone to intend it. It is simply the path of least resistance for a group under pressure. Over time, the person who absorbs outcomes becomes the system's stabilizer, and the system begins to rely on that stabilization.

Commitment language can deepen the bind. "I said I would handle it" becomes not just a promise to try, but a promise for an outcome. If the conditions change, the promise remains. The person feels bound to a result that was never fully theirs to deliver. The commitment becomes a moral claim, and the moral claim makes it difficult to release the outcome even when the outcome is clearly beyond control.

It does not take malice to create this. Most people are dealing with their own constraints, their own pressures, their own incomplete visibility. They are grateful when someone else can hold what they cannot. The gratitude is real, but it does not change the structure. When the outcome arrives, it still lands on you because you were the one who held the uncertainty.

Silence can also come from politeness. People may not want to argue with a person who is taking responsibility. They may not want to correct the narrative because the narrative makes their own position easier. If you are already blaming yourself, others do not have to decide where the responsibility lies. They can accept your ownership and move on. The outcome becomes settled not because it was correct, but because it was convenient.

This is how expectation drift turns into a habit. The habit is rewarded by speed and social ease. The person who assumes responsibility is praised for "stepping up." The system uses that stepping up as a new baseline. The person then becomes the default owner of outcomes that were never actually under their control.

Internal misinterpretation of effort magnifies it further. Effort is not only a means; it becomes a moral signal. If you care, you try. If you try, you expect a proportional return. The expectation is rarely stated, but it lives inside the feeling of fairness. When the return does not arrive, the mind does not question the structure; it questions the self. The effort becomes evidence, and the missing outcome becomes a verdict.

Over time, this creates a quiet, relentless accounting. Every extra hour, every sacrifice, every delay becomes a deposit that is waiting for a return. When the return is late or absent, the nervous system reads it as theft. This is not a logical conclusion; it is an emotional one. The body interprets the gap as a violation. That sensation then becomes part of the story of self: I gave, therefore I should have received.

Effort also becomes a defense. If you have worked hard, you feel safer when an outcome goes wrong, because you can point to the work. But that defense has a hidden cost: it reinforces the belief that the outcome is connected to your effort in the first place. The defense turns into proof of ownership.

This is why exhaustion does not always reduce responsibility. Sometimes exhaustion increases it. The more you have given, the more personal the outcome feels. The more personal it feels, the less you can allow yourself to disengage. You end up trapped in a loop where effort increases ownership and ownership increases effort.

Emotional fatigue builds without accusation. There is no clear person to blame, so the weight defaults inward. The fatigue is not a dramatic burnout at first. It is a low, steady depletion. You feel more tired after a good outcome than you used to feel after a bad one. You feel relief, not joy, when things go well. The nervous system is not celebrating; it is bracing for the next demand.

Rest begins to feel suspect. If outcomes are yours, rest feels like negligence. If results are not secured, rest feels like denial. Even when you are exhausted, you can feel as if you have not earned the right to stop. The internal voice becomes a supervisor that never leaves. It does not shout; it simply keeps the ledger open.

The cost is not only exhaustion. It is also a narrowing of attention. When you are carrying outcomes, you look for threats, for signals, for early warnings. You monitor your environment for indicators that the outcome is veering off course. That vigilance can look like care, but it functions like anxiety. It makes the world feel like a fragile system that you must hold together.

Over time, this vigilance becomes identity. You begin to describe yourself as someone who "handles" things, someone who "keeps it together." The description sounds strong, but it is built on the assumption that if you do not hold everything, everything will fall. That is a heavy story to live inside.

The internal voice that accompanies this story can be relentless. It reviews the past in search of a missed signal. It replays conversations with the goal of locating the precise moment the outcome could have changed. These replays do not always feel like worry; they can feel like responsibility. The difference is subtle. In both cases, the outcome is treated as yours to account for, and the mind conducts its audit accordingly.

The search for causal moments often produces counterfactuals. You imagine what would have happened if you had said one sentence differently, answered one message sooner, taken one different path. The counterfactuals multiply because the mind needs proof that the outcome was preventable. The proof restores a sense of agency, but it does so by placing the burden back on you.

Because the burden is internal, it is also private. You can be surrounded by people who understand the complexity of the situation and still feel alone with the outcome. Their reassurance may feel kind but insufficient, because it does not alter the internal ledger. The narrative of ownership is not easily displaced by external words. It lives in the structure of how you have learned to interpret events.

This is why carrying outcomes can be invisible to others. On the outside, you look capable. On the inside, you are managing a constant evaluation. You may not share that evaluation because it sounds unreasonable, even to you. But the silence only deepens the impression that the responsibility is yours. If it were not yours, you would not feel it so strongly. That is the internal logic, and it is persuasive.

The result is a narrowing of emotional range. Joy is tempered by the awareness that it might not last. Pride is cautious because it may invite a future failure. Relief replaces celebration because the outcome felt like a test that you barely passed. The emotional response becomes oriented toward control rather than experience.

Even positive outcomes are processed as evidence that you managed to hold the system together, rather than as events that occurred within a larger field.

Time itself begins to feel like a series of tests. The future feels like a schedule of outcomes that must be managed. The past feels like a list of results that must be accounted for. The present becomes a staging area, a place to prevent the next failure. The mind does not rest because it is always preparing to carry what might arrive.

This is not only exhausting; it can also feel lonely. The more you carry, the more you assume others are not carrying. You become the one who notices the loose thread, the potential risk, the unresolved consequence. That noticing becomes part of your identity. It feels necessary. It may even feel like care. But it is still a form of outcome ownership, and it narrows the space for ease.

This chapter is not an argument against responsibility. It is an argument against a specific confusion: the confusion between being involved and being in control. Involvement can exist without authority. Caring can exist without ownership. Decisions can exist without authorship. These distinctions are easy to name and hard to live, because the world rarely emphasizes them. It rewards the appearance of control and punishes ambiguity, even when ambiguity is the truth.

If the boundary is never shown, it is crossed by default. Once crossed, it is rarely questioned, only endured. The result is a life where outcomes feel personal even when they are not, where effort feels like a vow, and where the mind treats variance as a moral signal. That structure is not chosen, but it is lived.

Most people assume that the discomfort they feel after an unfavorable outcome is a signal to improve. Often it is not. Often it is the residue of an invisible overreach: a responsibility taken where no authority existed. That residue feels like conscience, so it is trusted. But it is not always conscience. It is sometimes the echo of a boundary that was never drawn.

That echo can be strong because it is familiar. It resembles the internal voice that has guided effort for years. It sounds like duty, like care, like seriousness. The familiarity makes it persuasive. Yet the feeling persists even when the situation is clearly beyond any one person's control. The persistence is the sign that the feeling is not necessarily about the outcome itself, but about the long habit of interpreting outcomes as personal. The habit is what remains when the facts do not fit.

The chapters that follow do not aim to correct this instinct. They aim to expose the structure that created it. Not to demand different action, but to make visible what was never actually being held.

Chapter 2

Effort Without Response Is Not a Personal Failure

There is a particular kind of exhaustion that comes from doing everything you can think to do, and watching nothing move.

It is not the exhaustion of hard work. It is not the tiredness of long hours. It is the fatigue of throwing effort into a space that does not answer.

When response is absent, the mind rushes to make sense of the absence. It wants a cause. It wants a location for the failure. The most convenient location is the person who acted.

This is where a private story begins: if no one responds, it must be because the effort was insufficient. If nothing changes, it must be because the person did something wrong.

But lack of response is not proof of personal deficiency. It is often a reflection of how systems behave under load, under noise, and under attention limits.

The mismatch between effort and feedback is not a moral verdict. It is a structural feature of how results appear.

Response is not a direct return on effort. It is not a linear equation. It is an emergent property of many variables converging at once.

The person who acts feels the effort from the inside: intention, preparation, energy, and risk. The system receives the act from the outside: another signal among signals, another request among requests, another attempt among attempts.

The interior experience is dense. The exterior reception is thin.

This is not because the system is cruel. It is because the system is crowded.

A letter sent into a crowded room cannot know the crowd. It carries the weight of its own creation but is received with the weight of the room.

This mismatch is easy to forget, because effort is always accompanied by a sense of investment. Investment feels like it deserves a reply. When none arrives, the feeling becomes personal.

People do not only seek response as a practical indicator. They seek it as a social signal.

Response means recognition. Response means the other side has acknowledged that the effort exists. Response means that what happened has a place in shared reality.

Silence does not merely say that nothing happened. Silence says nothing at all. It denies the effort a location.

This is why silence is so potent. It forces the actor to choose between two interpretations: either the effort failed, or the effort never registered.

In most contexts, the second possibility is more unsettling than the first. Failure at least implies contact. Silence implies invisibility.

Invisibility is easy to internalize as unworthiness.

Yet invisibility is common in systems that filter by scarcity.

The scarcity is not only of time. It is also of attention, relevance, immediacy, and perceived risk. Most systems cannot afford to respond to everything they receive. They must sort, defer, or ignore.

Sorting is not a judgment of the sender. It is a function of the receiver's constraints.

A decision to ignore can be a decision to survive.

This is uncomfortable to accept because it separates response from meaning. It says that your effort can be seen and still not be answered. It says that your effort can be good and still not be acted on. It says that your effort can be necessary and still remain unacknowledged.

These are not moral statements. They are operational ones.

Many people want to believe that effort is legible. That if they try hard enough, the system will understand how hard they tried. That if they invest more, the response will eventually arrive.

This belief is not childish. It is a way to protect the relationship between action and self-worth.

If effort guarantees response, then response becomes a dependable measure of self. If effort does not guarantee response, then response loses that role. The self is left without a stable mirror.

This is why the absence of response can feel like an existential threat. It is not only about the outcome. It is about the disappearance of a reliable reflection.

The mind wants to recover the reflection by increasing effort. It wants to prove itself into existence.

But increased effort does not always increase response. It can also increase the sense of desperation, and desperation can be invisible to the system or misread by it.

The system sees volume, not motive. It sees frequency, not care. It sees a pattern, not a person.

When silence persists, escalation often follows. The person acts again, and again, changing the angle, changing the tone, adding more detail, making the signal louder.

The escalation is not always visible to others. It often happens internally, as a growing intensity of attention. The person starts to carry the situation everywhere, monitoring it, rehearsing it, feeling it behind every other task.

The system does not feel this escalation. It feels only a repeated signal. Repetition can be interpreted as urgency, or as noise. The difference depends on factors the person cannot control.

This is one of the quiet tragedies of effort without response. The person experiences escalation as increased care. The system experiences escalation as increased volume. These are not the same.

Silence also invites reinterpretation by observers.

Observers rarely have access to the internal effort. They see only the outcome, or the lack of it. They see a proposal with no adoption, an idea with no uptake, a request with no answer. It is natural to assume that if there was value, there would have been a response.

This assumption is a common error. It conflates visibility with worth.

In environments where response is scarce, worth often travels through bottlenecks. The bottleneck does not measure the sender; it measures the receiver's capacity. Yet observers often treat the bottleneck as a neutral judge.

The result is a subtle misinterpretation: lack of response is taken as evidence that the effort was misplaced, or that the person misread the situation. The person is seen as overreaching rather than the system being saturated.

Misinterpretation has consequences. It reduces the willingness of others to engage, which can further reduce response, reinforcing the appearance of low value. A loop forms, not because the effort is faulty, but because perception is self-reinforcing.

This loop is especially strong in contexts where response is treated as the only visible metric.

When response is the metric, silence becomes indistinguishable from failure. The world of effort collapses into the world of outcomes. The person is assessed by what the system chooses to show.

This creates a peculiar moral effect. The person is held responsible not only for the effort, but for the system's decision to notice or ignore it. The burden of attention shifts onto the actor, even though attention is not within the actor's authority.

The result is a quiet injustice. It looks like fair evaluation because it is anchored to results. But the results are filtered by forces outside the actor.

The more opaque the system, the more plausible the injustice.

In this environment, effort becomes a kind of risk.

It is not only the risk of failure. It is the risk of being misread. It is the risk that sincere effort will be interpreted as incompetence, that careful work will be interpreted as unnecessary, that patience will be interpreted as slowness, that persistence will be interpreted as fixation.

The person cannot easily correct these interpretations because the absence of response deprives them of a channel to do so.

Silence collapses nuance. It makes all efforts look the same from the outside: unproductive, invisible, or irrelevant.

This is why lack of response so often carries shame. Shame is not only about failure; it is about being mis-seen. It is about being rendered into a simple, negative category that does not fit the internal experience.

The internal experience is almost always more complex.

There are often genuine constraints. The person may have acted with partial information, under time pressure, within competing obligations, or with limited authority. The effort may have been high precisely because the environment was unstable.

If response does not arrive, the person may revise the narrative toward personal inadequacy, because it is the only narrative that gives a sense of control. If the problem is personal, it can be fixed. If the problem is systemic, it feels unmovable.

But the difference between personal and systemic is not a matter of blame. It is a matter of scope. Some situations are larger than individual effort, and response is mediated by factors that do not align with individual intention.

To mistake scope for self is to make a practical phenomenon into a moral judgment.

Consider the ordinary act of bringing a concern forward in a large organization.

The person prepares, gathers evidence, and frames the issue. The effort is careful. The response is delayed or absent. The person waits, then sends another message, then another. Months pass. The concern remains.

From the inside, the effort feels substantial. From the system, the concern is one of many, filtered through shifting priorities, calendar constraints, and decision fatigue. No single person feels responsible for the silence, and so the silence persists.

Later, the absence of response is used to suggest that the concern was not serious. It was raised, but apparently not important. The lack of response becomes retroactive evidence of insignificance.

Yet the significance did not change. What changed was the system's capacity to reflect it.

This is the central distortion: response is treated as a mirror of value, when it is often just a mirror of bandwidth.

The same distortion appears in publishing, in public discourse, in job seeking, in creative work, and in relationships.

A manuscript can be strong and still not find a reader at the right time. A proposal can be sound and still not make it onto the agenda. A message can be thoughtful and still land while the other side is overwhelmed.

The silence that follows is not a verdict on quality. It is often a timing outcome, a capacity outcome, a context outcome.

This does not make the silence pleasant. It does not remove disappointment. But it changes what the silence means.

When meaning changes, self-blame loosens.

Response is also shaped by the intersection of power and attention.

Those with authority can decide what counts as relevant. Their attention is the gate through which response passes. People without authority can work hard and still remain outside the gate, not because the work is poor, but because the gate is not designed to open for them.

This dynamic is not always visible. It can be disguised by polite language, by delays, by deferral, by procedural requirements that feel neutral. The person without authority experiences the neutrality as silence.

The person with authority may not even experience it as silence; they experience it as triage.

This asymmetry can be mistaken for personal inadequacy. It is, instead, a reflection of how authority shapes attention.

Effort without response is not only about external silence. It is also about internal echo.

When no one answers, the person often answers themselves. They replay the effort, analyze it, and imagine alternate versions. They interrogate their own motives, tone, and competence. The effort becomes an object of repeated scrutiny.

This internal echo feels like responsibility. It feels like taking the situation seriously. It feels like moral diligence.

But internal echo is not a reliable measure of external impact. It is a measure of how much uncertainty the person has to carry alone.

Uncertainty expands when response is absent. It spills into self-assessment, and the person begins to treat uncertainty as evidence of personal fault.

This is a common misinterpretation. Uncertainty is often a structural byproduct of silence.

The urge to resolve uncertainty by increasing effort can be intense.

More details, more research, more follow-up, more proof. The person tries to close the gap by adding weight to the signal.

Sometimes this works. Sometimes it does not. The problem is that even when it works, it does not reveal the underlying mechanism. The person can believe that the added effort caused the response, when it may have been timing, politics, or simple chance.

This creates a dangerous lesson: that effort must constantly escalate to secure a response. The person internalizes an ever-rising threshold.

A system with rising thresholds is not a system the individual can outrun. It is a system that consumes effort and never acknowledges its full cost.

This is why effort without response becomes a form of depletion rather than a path to resolution.

Depletion is not always visible to others.

The person continues to function, continues to appear engaged, continues to deliver. The hidden drain is the emotional labor of carrying unanswered attempts. Each attempt that went unanswered remains active in the mind, like an open loop.

Open loops are heavy. They require mental storage. They require vigilance. They invite self-criticism.

When others evaluate the person, they rarely see the open loops. They see only the present output. If the output falters, they interpret it as slowness or decline, not as the accumulated weight of unanswered effort.

The person's inner story becomes more burdened, while the outer evaluation becomes less forgiving. The distance between inner effort and outer response widens.

This is the quiet accumulation of unfairness.

There is also a temporal distortion in effort without response.

Response often arrives late, if it arrives at all. When it arrives late, it does not necessarily align with the original effort. The person may have already moved on, or they may have expended more effort in the absence of response. The response lands in a different context and is interpreted through that new context.

Late response can feel like a mixed message. It can feel like the system is finally acknowledging the effort, or it can feel like the system is reacting to a different version of the person.

In either case, the response does not repair the gap. It becomes another ambiguous signal to interpret.

Ambiguity invites more effort, which can restart the cycle.

In many environments, response is not only scarce but selective in ways that are difficult to predict.

A small gesture can receive immediate acknowledgment, while a major effort receives none. A casual remark can be amplified, while a carefully prepared statement disappears. This inconsistency is a feature of human attention, not a defect of the individual effort.

The unpredictability is destabilizing because it removes the ability to use response as a stable measure. The person cannot easily infer what the system values or how it decides.

In the absence of a stable measure, the person may default to self-critique, because it is the only variable that seems available.

This is the moment where the system's randomness becomes the person's shame.

Misinterpretation by observers can become more pronounced when the person escalates after silence.

Escalation can appear as obsession, even when it is simply persistence. It can appear as noise, even when it is simply effort. It can appear as overreaction, even when it is simply a response to long neglect.

Observers tend to attribute escalation to personality rather than to context. They see intensity and assume the person is intense by nature. They see repetition and assume the person is stubborn. They see urgency and assume the person lacks judgment.

These interpretations are easy and often wrong. They ignore the prior silence that provoked the escalation. They treat the person's behavior as if it emerged in a vacuum.

When the prior silence is invisible, the person is misread. Misreading becomes part of the story, and the person is asked to carry it.

This misreading can also travel backward in time.

Once a person is classified as someone who "overreacts" or "pushes too hard," their previous efforts are reinterpreted through that lens. What was once seen as diligence becomes seen as compulsion. What was once seen as care becomes seen as control.

This retroactive reclassification deepens the sense of personal failure. The person is not only blamed for the absence of response, but also for the effort that preceded it.

The weight of this is not small. It makes the person doubt their own perception. It makes them question whether their effort was legitimate or misguided.

Yet the original condition remains: response was absent, and the person was left to interpret the absence alone.

Silence also has a way of collapsing distinctions between kinds of effort.

An effort that is exploratory, tentative, or speculative is treated the same as an effort that is decisive or urgent. Without response, the system offers no feedback about which kind of effort was received.

The person loses the ability to differentiate the categories of their own action.

When all efforts yield the same response, or lack of response, the person is tempted to conclude that none of them mattered. This conclusion is not always accurate, but it becomes plausible through repetition.

The danger is not only demoralization. The danger is the internalization of a false model of cause and effect.

That model says: effort does not matter. Or effort matters only if it is extreme. Or effort matters only if it is performed by someone else.

These conclusions distort the landscape. They are born not of evidence, but of absence.

Lack of response can also be influenced by the invisibility of the work itself.

Some efforts are quiet by nature. They prevent problems rather than solving visible ones. They stabilize environments before instability becomes obvious. They reduce risk without producing a visible artifact.

Such efforts are particularly vulnerable to silence because their success is measured by the absence of events. When nothing goes wrong, there is nothing to respond to.

The person who performs this work is often praised only when something fails. Silence, in this context, is the default response to success.

This creates a paradox: the better the effort, the more invisible it becomes. The invisibility can be interpreted as insignificance, when it is actually a sign of effectiveness.

The person, seeing no response, may begin to undervalue the very work that keeps the system stable.

Even when effort is visible, it can be rendered invisible by scale.

In large systems, individual contributions are absorbed into collective outcomes. The outcome is acknowledged, but the individual effort is not. This is not always malicious. It is a consequence of scale. Recognition is more expensive than action.

When a person is part of a large effort, the silence around individual contribution can feel like erasure. The person may begin to believe that their effort did not matter.

Yet the absence of recognition does not negate the contribution. It only means that the system's recognition mechanism cannot scale to match the effort.

Again, the absence of response reflects system behavior rather than personal deficiency.

There is also the phenomenon of delayed recognition without retroactive repair.

A system might eventually respond, but the response arrives without acknowledgment of the time and uncertainty that preceded it. The response answers the content, but not the experience. It does not address the months of silence, the internal echo, the repeated attempts.

From the system's perspective, the response is complete. From the person's perspective, it is incomplete.

This mismatch can be destabilizing. The person is asked to treat the response as full closure, but their lived experience does not align. They carry the residue of silence even after a reply arrives.

The silence leaves a mark that response alone does not erase.

In conversations about effort, there is a tendency to equate persistence with virtue.

Persistence is often celebrated. Yet persistence in the face of silence is not always virtuous; it can be a form of compulsion induced by uncertainty. The moral framing of persistence can trap people into misreading their own motives.

If persistence is treated as inherently good, then stopping becomes morally suspect. The person feels compelled to continue not because the effort is effective, but because the moral framing makes discontinuation feel like failure.

This is another way that silence becomes personal. The system's lack of response induces a moral narrative inside the person, which then overrides practical considerations.

The system does not demand this narrative. The person constructs it to fill the void.

There is also a social layer to silence.

In group settings, the absence of response can be used to maintain hierarchy. Silence can be a way to avoid granting legitimacy. It can be a way to keep someone outside the circle of acknowledged contributors. It can be a way to avoid the political cost of saying no.

When silence is used in this way, it is not a personal critique. It is a tactic, even if it is unspoken. It is a way to manage the distribution of recognition and influence.

The person who experiences this silence may interpret it as personal failure, because the tactic is invisible. They do not see the boundary, only the absence.

This is how power hides inside non-response. It uses silence to avoid accountability while still shaping the field of action.

Silence can also be a byproduct of conflict avoidance.

People often avoid responding because response would create friction. Saying yes creates commitment. Saying no creates confrontation. Silence preserves ambiguity and defers the emotional cost.

In this case, the silence is not about the effort at all. It is about the respondent's reluctance to engage in a difficult interaction. The effort becomes collateral to that reluctance.

The person who acted is likely to interpret the silence as a judgment of their effort, because the true cause is hidden. They are left to infer from absence, and the inference tends to fall on the self.

Again, the system behavior is not a mirror of personal deficiency. It is a mirror of human avoidance.

The repeated experience of silence can create a subtle shift in identity.

The person begins to see themselves as someone whose efforts do not land. This identity is not chosen; it is inferred. It is inferred from the pattern of non-response and then reinforced by it.

Once this identity forms, the person may interpret future silence as confirmation, even when the silence has different causes. The narrative becomes self-sustaining.

This is a powerful psychological trap. It turns situational outcomes into stable self-concepts.

The exit from this trap is not a simple action. It is a change in interpretation, and interpretation is not easily willed.

What matters here is the recognition that the identity is built on a fragile foundation: the behavior of systems that do not respond.

Effort without response is especially destabilizing when the effort involved risk.

When someone takes a risk, they expect some form of acknowledgment, even if it is a negative response. Risk is a bid to be seen. Silence makes the risk feel wasted, and it can make the person question the legitimacy of taking risks at all.

This is not about fear. It is about meaning. Risk without response can feel like self-exposure without validation.

The person may conclude that they misjudged the environment. They may conclude that they misjudged themselves. These conclusions are understandable, but they do not necessarily follow.

Risk is not always followed by response. That is a property of risky environments, not of flawed individuals.

In many professional settings, the expectation of response is framed as part of a feedback culture.

Feedback cultures promise responsiveness, but they often cannot deliver it. They are aspirational. The discrepancy between the promise and the lived experience can intensify self-blame. If the culture is supposed to respond and it does not, then the person assumes the problem lies within them.

This is the danger of ideals that outrun capacity. They turn system limitations into personal shortcomings.

The person is not wrong to want feedback. The person is wrong only if they interpret its absence as proof of unworthiness.

The system is wrong if it pretends that responsiveness is guaranteed.

There is a common belief that good work will eventually be recognized.

Sometimes it is. Sometimes it is not. Recognition is a social process, not a law of nature. It depends on visibility, on alignment, on timing, and on narrative. It is not a pure function of quality.

When recognition does not arrive, it is tempting to reinterpret the work as bad. This reinterpretation is a way to restore causal order, but it can be false.

It is also tempting to reinterpret the self as inadequate. This, too, restores causal order, but it does so by placing the burden on the person rather than on the conditions.

The more honest interpretation is that recognition is conditional and uneven. That unevenness does not map cleanly onto individual worth.

There is also the matter of competing signals.

In a saturated environment, signals compete for attention. The system may respond to a signal not because it is the best, but because it is the loudest, the closest, the most familiar, or the most aligned with current priorities. The person who sends a careful, nuanced signal may lose to a less careful one simply because it lands at the right time.

This does not mean that careful effort is wrong. It means that response is not a neutral evaluator.

If the person interprets the lack of response as a judgment on their care, they misattribute the cause. The cause is often the competition for attention, not the inadequacy of the effort.

The presence of competition is a system property. It is not a personal verdict.

Silence can also be a function of organizational memory.

Organizations forget. They forget what was promised, what was attempted, what was documented. They do not remember the effort, because effort was not recorded in the channels that the organization recognizes.

When the organization forgets, the person feels erased. They may then interpret the erasure as a failure of their effort, when it is actually a failure of the system's memory.

This is another way that systems convert effort into invisibility.

The person may respond by making their effort more visible, but visibility is not always available, and it is not always safe. The lack of response remains.

Here again, the absence of response is not a measure of personal worth. It is a measure of institutional attention.

The emotional consequence of these patterns is often confusion.

Confusion is not only about what happened; it is about what it means. When response is inconsistent, the person cannot reliably infer how the system evaluates effort. The person is left with ambiguous data and high stakes.

In such conditions, the mind looks for stable explanations. It chooses explanations that are close at hand. The self is always close at hand.

This is why personal blame is so common. It is the most available explanation, not the most accurate.

To say that lack of response reflects system behavior is not to dismiss personal responsibility. It is to situate it correctly. It is to say that personal effort exists within larger patterns that shape what is seen and what is ignored.

This is the de-blaming move: to relocate the meaning of silence away from personal deficiency and toward the mechanics of attention, authority, and capacity.

The mechanics are rarely visible to the person who is acting.

They are not visible because systems do not announce their thresholds. They do not reveal how many requests are waiting. They do not reveal who else is competing for attention. They do not reveal how decisions are made in the moment.

The person operates in partial information. They send effort into a dark room.

If the room remains dark, the person does not know whether the effort failed, whether it was unseen, or whether it was deferred. Silence is indistinguishable across these possibilities.

In such a context, self-critique becomes the easiest narrative. It can be rehearsed without new data. It can be intensified without new input.

Yet the absence of new input is precisely the problem. The person is trapped in a loop of interpretation without external correction.

When a system finally responds, the response can be misaligned with the person's accumulated meaning.

The response might be brief, procedural, or purely transactional. It might treat the effort as routine. It might ignore the emotional cost of the silence. The person, having carried the effort internally for a long time, feels the response as an underreaction.

This underreaction can be experienced as disrespect, but it is often a result of scale. The system is not equipped to respond to the person as a full context; it responds to the request as a unit of work.

The person may then interpret the response as a judgment on their worth, because the response seems to minimize what they experienced.

Here again, the mismatch is structural. It is not a statement about personal value.

There is a related phenomenon: the over-response.

Sometimes, after long silence, the system responds with sudden intensity. The issue becomes urgent. The person is asked to act quickly. The system behaves as if the effort was obvious all along.

This can create a sense of whiplash. The person may feel vindicated, but also exploited. Their earlier effort was ignored; now it is treated as self-evident, and the burden is returned to them in a compressed timeline.

The over-response reveals that the system did not lack capacity in general. It lacked capacity at the time, or lacked willingness to acknowledge. The person's effort becomes contingent on momentary attention.

The lesson is not that effort is futile. The lesson is that response is episodic, and its timing is not under individual control.

Effort without response often occurs in environments that reward visible wins.

In such environments, the visible win becomes a proxy for merit, and the invisible effort becomes irrelevant. People learn to associate worth with visibility, not with substance.

The person who invests in substance without immediate visibility can be misjudged, even when their work is foundational. Their effort is not aligned with the system's reward cues.

This mismatch can lead to internal conflict. The person may feel that their values are intact but their outcomes are lacking. The silence becomes a signal that values are out of sync with the environment.

This is a painful position. It tempts the person to rewrite their values to fit the system. It tempts them to equate response with worth.

The de-blaming perspective resists this temptation. It insists that lack of response does not rewrite the value of the effort.

Observer misinterpretation can also arise from cultural narratives about meritocracy.

In a meritocratic story, outcomes are treated as the natural result of effort and talent. Silence becomes evidence that effort was insufficient or talent was lacking. The story is simple and appealing.

But the story is often wrong. It ignores bottlenecks, gatekeepers, timing, and the randomness of attention. It ignores the ways in which systems privilege certain kinds of signals over others.

When observers apply the meritocratic story, they misread the absence of response as proof of a lack within the person. This misreading is not malicious; it is inherited.

The person who experiences silence thus carries not only the silence, but also the weight of a cultural narrative that interprets silence as personal failure.

The difficulty is not only practical. It is interpretive. It is a clash between lived complexity and inherited simplicity.

It is important to distinguish between effort that is ineffective and effort that is unacknowledged.

Ineffective effort exists, and it can be improved. But unacknowledged effort can be strong and still unseen. The two are not equivalent, yet they are often treated as the same because both lead to the same outward result: no response.

The conflation of these two creates unnecessary self-doubt. It also creates distorted evaluations by others.

The person cannot fully resolve this conflation because the system does not provide enough feedback to separate the categories. The absence of response collapses them into one.

This is why the absence of response is so potent as a generator of self-blame. It hides the difference between failure and invisibility.

The de-blaming move is to keep that difference alive, even when the system does not.

Some people respond to silence by withdrawing. Others respond by intensifying effort. Both responses are shaped by the same lack of information.

Withdrawal can look like apathy. Intensification can look like obsession. Observers may interpret these behaviors as personality traits, but they are often responses to the same structural condition: a system that does not answer.

The interpretation matters because it shapes future treatment. If withdrawal is read as laziness, the person is marginalized further. If intensification is read as neediness, the person is dismissed further. In both cases, the system's silence is converted into a story about the person.

This is the reinforcing loop: silence generates behavior, behavior is misread, misreading reduces response, which deepens silence.

Breaking this loop is not a matter of a simple act. It requires a shift in how silence is interpreted, both by the person and by observers.

The most difficult aspect of effort without response is the ambiguity of accountability.

In some contexts, the person truly is responsible for the outcome. In others, the person is merely responsible for the effort. The line between these two forms of responsibility is not always clear. Silence obscures it further.

When the line is unclear, people tend to assume they are responsible for outcomes, because it is safer to assume too much responsibility than too little. This is a common moral reflex.

But excessive responsibility produces distorted self-assessment. It leads people to absorb outcomes that are not under their control. It transforms system behavior into personal guilt.

The de-blaming perspective acknowledges responsibility for effort without collapsing it into responsibility for response.

There is a subtle difference between being ignored and being refused.

Refusal is painful, but it is a form of engagement. It says, at minimum, that the effort was seen. It gives the person a clear point of contact. It allows the effort to be placed in context.

Silence offers no such placement. It keeps the effort in limbo. It denies the person the clarity of a no.

This is why silence feels worse than rejection. Rejection has a shape. Silence is shapeless.

The absence of shape invites interpretation, and interpretation often lands on the self.

To recognize silence as a system behavior is to recognize that its shapelessness is not a statement about the person. It is a statement about the system's inability or unwillingness to engage.

The experience of effort without response can also distort time.

The person spends time waiting, time revisiting, time explaining, time trying again. This time is not always visible to others. The effort appears to be a single act, but it is actually a sustained occupation of attention.

When the system finally responds, it does not account for the time spent in waiting. It responds to the initial act, not the ongoing occupation. The person feels unseen, even in response.

This is an important nuance. Lack of response is not only about lack of acknowledgment of the act. It is about lack of acknowledgment of the duration of the effort.

When duration is unseen, the person is more likely to feel that their effort was wasted. The system, however, is not designed to recognize duration. It is designed to process discrete requests.

Again, the mismatch is structural.

Effort without response also interacts with memory in a particular way.

When responses are rare, they become weighted. The person remembers each one, not only for its content but for its rarity. The scarcity of response makes each response feel like a verdict on the self.

This is a heavy load for a single moment to carry. A brief reply becomes a sign of hope or a sign of dismissal. The person reads deeply into a few words because those words are the only data available.

The system does not intend to carry this weight. It sends the reply for practical reasons, not to provide a psychological anchor. The person, however, needs the anchor.

This asymmetry adds to the sense of personal failure. The person begins to treat system noise as personal message.

In social contexts, response is also entangled with affiliation.

People respond more readily to those they know, those they trust, those they perceive as similar. This is not necessarily favoritism; it is the ordinary economy of social attention.

For someone outside those circles, silence can feel like a personal deficit. In reality, it may be a signal of distance rather than deficiency. The effort is not ignored because it is bad, but because the social connection is thin.

This does not make the silence less painful. It does, however, relocate its meaning. It is about the thickness of relationship, not the worth of the effort.

This is another example of how lack of response reflects system behavior rather than personal deficiency.

The de-blaming perspective is not a refusal of responsibility. It is a refusal to accept responsibility for what the system does not acknowledge.

It recognizes that systems have constraints, that attention is scarce, that response is filtered, and that silence often signals capacity limits rather than personal inadequacy.

This perspective does not promise comfort. It does not guarantee results. It does not provide a method for securing response. It simply corrects the attribution of meaning.

When meaning is corrected, the emotional burden shifts. The person can see that the absence of response is not necessarily about their worth. It is often about the system's boundaries.

This shift is subtle. It does not eliminate disappointment. But it removes the extra layer of self-reproach that comes from assuming personal failure.

There are domains where response is structurally unlikely, even when effort is essential.

Care work is a clear example. Much of its value is expressed in what does not happen: crises avoided, harm reduced, stability maintained. The system that benefits from this work often lacks a mechanism to respond in proportion to the care given. The caregiver is left with a silence that can easily be misread as indifference or as a signal that the work is unnecessary, when in fact the work is the reason nothing broke.

The same logic appears in maintenance, in safety, in governance, and in any role that is tasked with preventing failure rather than producing visible success. The effort sits in the background; the response is reserved for moments of breakdown. Silence becomes the normal state, and the person is asked to interpret a lack of acknowledgment as neutral. Yet neutral silence is not experienced as neutral by the person who carries the effort.

This is another place where the system's response fails to mirror the value of the effort. The mismatch is not a flaw in the person. It is a feature of work that is designed to make itself invisible.

To understand effort without response is to understand the asymmetry between agency and acknowledgment.

Agency is experienced internally. Acknowledgment is granted externally. The two do not always meet. When they do not meet, the person experiences a gap that cannot be closed by effort alone.

The gap is not a sign that the person is insufficient. It is a sign that agency and acknowledgment operate on different logics.

The temptation is to equate the absence of acknowledgment with the absence of agency. That equation is false. Agency can be real even when it is unrecognized.

This is the core claim. It is a claim about the structure of response, not about the character of the person.

The chapter's role is de-blame. De-blame does not mean denial of consequences. It means refusing to internalize a system's silence as a moral verdict.

The effort still exists. The effort still carries meaning. The effort still shapes the person's identity and experience. But it does not necessarily shape the system's response.

The distance between these two realities is not a personal failure. It is a feature of how complex environments absorb human action.

If there is a way to hold this, it is not through instruction, but through recognition. The person can see that the lack of response is not the only possible mirror of the self.

There are other mirrors: the integrity of the effort, the clarity of the intention, the care invested in the act. These are not substitutes for response, but they are different kinds of evidence.

They exist even when the system is silent.

When the system finally responds, or when it never does, the person still carries the effort.

The question is not whether the effort mattered, but what kind of mattering is being used to evaluate it.

If mattering is defined only by external response, then silence becomes definitive. If mattering can include the internal coherence of the effort, the alignment with one's values, the contribution to stability or understanding, then silence does not erase it.

This is not a recommendation. It is a description of two different evaluative frames. One is external and scarce. The other is internal and accessible.

Neither frame guarantees relief. But the existence of the second frame prevents the first from becoming total.

The most important point is simple: lack of response reflects system behavior, not personal deficiency.

Systems are noisy. They are selective. They are constrained. They do not respond to everything. They cannot.

People do not always see these constraints, and so they misread silence as personal failure. That misreading adds a burden that does not belong to them.

The burden is not a fair cost of effort. It is an extra cost created by a misattribution.

To remove that cost is not to deny disappointment. It is to prevent disappointment from becoming shame.

At the end of the silence, a question remains, not about what to do next, but about what the silence actually meant.

Was it a verdict on the effort, or a reflection of a system that could not answer?

The answer is rarely available in full. But the possibility itself is the beginning of de-blame.

At what point did a lack of response become a verdict on the self?

Chapter 3

When effort becomes a trap

Effort is one of the most socially reinforced behaviors.

From early on, we are taught that effort is neutral, even virtuous. If something fails, the remedy is simple: try harder.

This belief is so deeply embedded that it often survives direct contradiction. Even when increased effort produces no improvement, the reflex remains.

Try harder. Stay later. Think more carefully. Care more.

Effort is praised in classrooms, rewarded in evaluations, admired in stories of grit. It is visible in a way that judgment is not. It can be seen, measured, recounted, thanked. It also feels fair: if the person who tries hardest is honored, then the world seems legible. The idea that effort is always good becomes a moral fact rather than a practical one.

That moral status matters. It means effort is not only a tool but a public signal of character. It becomes a way to demonstrate loyalty, seriousness, and worth. So even when effort is misapplied, it still produces social returns. Those returns create a loop: effort earns praise; praise reinforces effort; effort feels safe.

The loop hides a different truth. Effort does not guarantee influence, and it does not grant control. It can cover for missing structure, but it cannot substitute for it. The more effort is treated as a default remedy, the more the underlying absence is allowed to persist.

Visibility explains some of the loyalty to effort. Effort leaves traces: time logged, messages sent, late nights noticed. Judgment leaves fewer traces, and authority leaves traces only when it is exercised. So effort becomes the easiest proxy for commitment. The proxy is comfortable because it can be quantified. If effort is the visible thing, then effort becomes the thing that is rewarded.

This creates a peculiar inversion of value. The person who clears obstacles is praised less than the person who stays up late with the obstacles. The person who makes a decisive call is noticed only if the call is dramatic. The person who keeps the wheels turning, even if the wheels should not be turning at all, is celebrated for endurance. The system learns to honor the presence of effort rather than the presence of alignment.

Effort is also safe to celebrate. Praising effort does not require taking a stance on whether the underlying structure makes sense. It avoids the discomfort of structural critique. It can be offered generously without the risk of redistributing power. So the praise flows freely while the structure stays fixed.

The personal and the structural separate here. The person may be doing everything right within the limits of their role. The role itself may be misaligned. Effort blurs that distinction and makes the misalignment feel like a personal shortcoming. The social rewards that come with effort then lock the person into the very role that produces the shortcoming. The system appears stable because the person is stable, not because the system is well designed.

Effort can also be deployed without comprehension. A person can work intensely on the wrong problem, or on a problem whose solution is outside their authority. Effort looks like movement even when it is stationary, like running in place. Because it is visible, it is often mistaken for progress. The praise comes for the visible motion rather than the invisible alignment.

A culture that venerates effort rarely distinguishes between energy and effectiveness. The two are emotionally linked, but structurally separate. Energy is personal; effectiveness is relational. Effectiveness depends on the ability to decide, to allocate, to redirect. If those powers are absent, effort becomes a mask for their absence.

There is also a historical residue in the praise of effort. Many social systems were built around scarcity and hardship. In those contexts, effort was often the most controllable variable. The myth that effort always solves problems made survival feel possible. That myth persists even when the problems have changed. The modern version of it is subtle: if you are exhausted, you must be doing the right thing.

Exhaustion becomes a badge of legitimacy. In competitive environments, it distinguishes the committed from the casual. In moral environments, it distinguishes the caring from the indifferent. The badge is worn not because suffering is valuable, but because suffering is convincing. It convinces others of sincerity. It convinces the person themselves that they are participating fully.

This is why effort can take on a ritual quality. There is a cadence to late nights, to quick replies, to visible busyness. The cadence reassures the group that the work is being handled. It reassures the person that they are worthy of their place. The reassurance is real, but it is expensive. It costs time, attention, and, eventually, the ability to distinguish between what is urgent and what is merely habitual.

Ritualized effort also narrows the space for judgment. If the group expects the ritual, then deviating from it feels like failure even when the deviation would be wise. Judgment becomes harder to express because it does not look like effort. It looks like pause, reflection, reconsideration. Those gestures are quieter, and quiet gestures are easy to misread.

This is one reason effort becomes so difficult to disentangle from responsibility. When effort is the social proof, then the person who reduces effort is interpreted as reducing responsibility. The interpretation is not fair, but it is common. It pushes the person toward continued exertion, even when exertion no longer addresses the real issue.

The moralization of effort adds a layer of guilt to any withdrawal. If effort is good, then reducing effort must be bad. The person who slows down is not simply resting; they are risking a moral downgrade. This is why effort has such durable power. It is not only a habit; it is a virtue.

At a certain point, effort stops being a tool and becomes an identity.

You are no longer someone who applies effort when appropriate. You are someone who is defined by effort.

And identities, once formed, resist revision.

The identity of the diligent person changes the meaning of absence. If effort is who you are, then a gap in the system is not simply a gap. It is an invitation to demonstrate the identity again. It is a moment to reaffirm the self.

This is not vanity; it is how social roles stabilize. Groups rely on recognizable patterns. The person who "always steps in" becomes the person who is expected to step in. Even when no one says it aloud, the expectation settles around them. It becomes part of the background, like furniture that no one remembers placing.

The identity also becomes a kind of shield. It protects against accusations of indifference and against the fear of being unnecessary. It allows a person to feel indispensable. But it also binds them to a role that was never formally defined.

Identity makes effort sticky. Once effort is associated with character, withdrawing effort feels like withdrawing the self. The social cost of inconsistency rises. So the effort continues, even when the situation no longer warrants it.

There is a quiet loneliness to this identity. The diligent person is appreciated, but not necessarily seen. What is seen is the output, the reliability, the rescue. What is not seen is the internal narrowing of possibility. The identity becomes a corridor: it creates a clear path but it also limits the field of movement.

Identity also shifts the perception of choice. If effort is who someone is, the line between choice and obligation fades. What begins as voluntary becomes expected, then assumed. The person may still feel in control, yet the pattern has hardened. They have a reputation to uphold, and reputation is a social contract.

In many environments, reputations are more stable than formal roles. Titles change; reputations linger. A person can move across teams and still be seen as the one who "gets it done." The reputation travels with them, and the work travels too. Responsibility can follow reputation faster than authority can follow title.

Reputation acts like a shadow form of authority. It grants access to requests and expectations, not to decisions. People consult the reliable person, not because that person has been formally empowered, but because they have been informally proven. The proof becomes a claim. The claim is exercised through proximity rather than through structure.

This makes the reliable person a magnet for unresolved issues. Requests accumulate because the reliable person is the safest place to put them. "Safe" here means predictable: the work will likely be done. Predictability is often valued more than fairness or formal alignment. So reputation becomes a route through which responsibility can travel quickly, bypassing authority entirely.

Reputation also changes the emotional economics of withdrawal. If someone is known for being dependable, a pause is interpreted as a break in character. The person may feel a need to preserve consistency, even when the underlying role has shifted without consent. The social contract is renewed each time they comply. Compliance becomes a vote for the structure as it exists.

There is a deeper psychological effect as well. When a person is recognized primarily for effort, effort begins to feel like the only stable identity available. Other identities are less acknowledged. The person is caught between the comfort of being needed and the cost of being defined by need. The reputation is flattering and restrictive at once.

The trap begins when effort is used to compensate for structural absence.

You exert effort to make up for missing clarity. You exert effort to stabilize unclear roles. You exert effort to bridge gaps in authority, ownership, or decision rights.

In the short term, this works.

The system continues to function. Outcomes are delayed rather than prevented. Conflicts are softened rather than resolved.

From the outside, the effort looks effective.

From the inside, it feels necessary.

The short-term success is what makes the trap sustainable. When someone covers a gap with effort, the consequences of the gap do not arrive. Without consequences, the structure does not change. The system learns that the gap is tolerable, even efficient.

What begins as an emergency measure becomes a stable expectation. A temporary patch becomes a permanent seam. The person applying effort becomes the unofficial owner of the problem. The role is never written down, but it exists in the minds of everyone who benefits from it.

Structural absence often starts small. It can be a vague responsibility, a missing decision, a policy that no longer fits. Because the absence is small, it feels reasonable for someone to fill it. But once it has been filled, the system adapts to the new normal. The patch becomes a part of the architecture.

This is how responsibility migrates faster than authority. The work moves downward, toward the person who absorbs it, while the formal right to decide remains above. The migration is informal, quiet, and often affectionate. No meeting is held, no title is changed, no authority is granted. Yet the responsibility arrives all the same.

This migration is not necessarily malicious. It is often the result of convenience, habit, and social economy. If someone already knows how to fix an issue, the simplest path is to ask them again. If someone already handled a situation, it feels natural to assume they will handle it next time. The system obeys gravity. Responsibility falls toward the person most likely to catch it.

That catch often begins with a small, apparently harmless act. A single rescue on a deadline becomes a precedent. A quick reply becomes a norm. A willingness to "jump in" becomes a definition of the role. The transfer is not announced; it is remembered. The memory becomes a standing instruction.

Informal expectation transfer is a method of coordination that does not feel like a method. It works by social recall rather than by formal assignment. People ask the person who did it last time, the person who knows the context, the person who is least likely to say no. The reason given is usually efficiency. The effect is usually reassignment.

Over time, the reason is forgotten and the reassignment remains. The person becomes the default, and the default becomes the explanation. "Because it has always been you" is not stated, but it is understood. The responsibility migrates not by instruction but by inertia.

This is why responsibility can spread through a system faster than authority can be granted. Formal authority requires a decision about who holds it, what it covers, and how it is monitored. Informal responsibility requires only a moment of need and a person who can meet it. The speed of need outpaces the speed of formal decision.

The pattern appears in small, ordinary scenes. A colleague forwards a confusing request with a note that says, "You know this stuff." A family member is asked to "just handle the details" because they are good at it. A friend group falls into the habit of letting one person plan because it goes smoothly. In each case, competence is treated as a reason to transfer responsibility. Authority does not follow; the person is expected to produce outcomes without the power to change the constraints.

Informality makes the transfer feel kind. It is framed as trust or gratitude. It is rarely framed as a shift in obligations. So the person receives the expectation without the chance to define its limits. They become responsible for coordination, for communication, for follow-through. They do not become authorized to change priorities, to change resources, or to change the timeline.

The person begins to do the work of authority without the title of authority. They make decisions in practice but cannot make decisions in name. They carry the burden of outcomes but cannot change the conditions that shape those outcomes. Their work becomes a private bridge over a public gap.

That gravity is intensified by scarcity. When authority is concentrated, it cannot move quickly enough to match the spread of responsibility. Authority is slow because it is bounded by formal structures. Responsibility is fast because it can move through informal expectations. The gap between them widens.

In that widening gap, a shadow structure emerges. Someone becomes the unofficial coordinator. They translate between groups, chase updates, resolve conflicts that are not theirs to resolve. They are relied on to interpret decisions they did not make. The organization appears smoother because their labor absorbs the friction.

This shadow structure is fragile. It exists in habits and personal memory, not in roles. It depends on one person staying in place. If that person leaves, the hidden infrastructure collapses and the formal structure is suddenly exposed. But while the person remains, the system has little incentive to formalize the role. The gap is being bridged, so the gap is treated as if it does not exist.

This is why hero narratives are common in such environments. The "hero" is the person who keeps things moving despite the lack of authority. The narrative celebrates the individual rather than the structure. It turns a systemic misalignment into a personal achievement. The celebration then protects the misalignment from critique.

The person who carries the shadow structure often becomes the point where accountability concentrates. They are the one who "knows," so they are the one who is asked. They are the one who is asked, so they are the one who is blamed. They hold the responsibility of authority without the protections of it.

Structural absence also hides in ambiguity. When ownership is unclear, tasks drift toward whoever seems most concerned. Concern is mistaken for mandate. The person who notices becomes the person responsible. The noticing is a sign of care, but it is interpreted as acceptance of the burden.

In small teams, this drift can feel like collaboration. Everyone helps; everyone pitches in. But over time, the drift consolidates. The person who fills the gap most often becomes the one who is expected to fill it always. Informality hardens into a role.

In larger organizations, the drift can be even more pronounced. Responsibilities cross boundaries, but authority remains siloed. A person is asked to coordinate across departments without the decision rights those departments possess. Their effort becomes the glue that holds a fragmented structure together. The glue is valued, but glue is not given authority over the pieces it holds.

The trap is not simply about working hard. It is about working hard in the absence of structural alignment. The person becomes a compensating mechanism. The system functions because someone is absorbing its missing parts. That absorption has a cost.

What is rarely acknowledged is that effort has no natural ceiling.

There is always more you could have done. Another message you could have sent. Another angle you could have considered. Another hour you could have stayed.

Because the boundary is undefined, the stopping rule becomes psychological rather than structural.

You stop not when the task is complete, but when you are depleted.

In domains where responsibility has migrated, completion is not a clear state. If a person is covering gaps that are not formally theirs, there is no formal "done." Each time the system stumbles, the same person can be called on. The ceiling is removed. Effort expands to fill whatever space exists.

This ceilinglessness is not only about time; it is about attention. The problem follows the person beyond the scheduled hours and beyond the formal scope. It moves into their thoughts, their background stress, their sense of vigilance. Because the responsibility was never granted, there is no shared agreement about its limits.

The effect is subtle. The person doing the work may still be praised, still be seen as a model of dedication. But the absence of boundaries means the praise is attached to an unbounded role. The role itself becomes elastic, stretching as far as the person can stretch.

Elastic roles create elastic days. Time that was once personal becomes time that is always potentially available. The person begins to monitor their own availability, scanning for messages, anticipating needs, preparing for contingencies. The work becomes anticipatory rather than reactive. Anticipation is exhausting because it never ends. There is always another possible failure to guard against, another thread to keep alive.

The elasticity also changes how risk is perceived. If the person is the one who will absorb the consequences, then every small risk feels personal. The system may tolerate uncertainty, but the person cannot. So they invest extra effort to reduce uncertainty, even when uncertainty is structurally inevitable. The extra effort is invisible, but the anxiety is real.

This is one way the ceiling disappears. The work is no longer about completing tasks; it is about preventing the next task from failing. Prevention has no finish line. It is defined by what does not happen. When nothing happens, it is ambiguous whether the prevention worked or the risk never existed. The person cannot know, so they keep preventing.

Ceilinglessness also changes the meaning of success. When a task has no defined endpoint, any pause looks like failure. Completion becomes an emotion rather than an outcome. If the person feels anxious, they interpret it as unfinished. If they feel relief, they interpret it as done. The task itself never declares its closure.

This is why effort can be self-perpetuating. The person does more, but the system does not adjust its expectations. The work becomes the water in which the person swims. It is no longer a discrete task; it is a constant condition.

The ceilinglessness is reinforced by the invisibility of certain kinds of work. When the work is about preventing problems rather than producing visible outputs, its success is the absence of events. The system does not notice absence. It notices only presence, the presence of effort, the presence of the person. So effort must continue to remain visible.

This is where effort turns against the person applying it.

The mind begins to equate exhaustion with responsibility fulfilled. Rest starts to feel suspicious. Disengagement feels like abandonment.

When outcomes remain unsatisfactory, the conclusion is predictable:

"I didn't try hard enough."

This conclusion is emotionally coherent—but structurally false.

Emotional coherence is powerful. It provides a simple explanation that preserves the moral order: if the outcome is poor, then more effort was needed. The alternative explanation is more threatening. It implies that the structure is misaligned, that authority has not been paired with responsibility, that the system is relying on sacrifice. Those implications are harder to face, so the mind returns to the familiar script.

The script is reinforced by others. People thank the person for "going above and beyond." They note how much is being carried. But they rarely shift the underlying structure that made the carrying necessary. Praise becomes a compensation for what is missing. The person is celebrated for endurance rather than supported by authority.

Over time, endurance becomes the only available form of success. If the problem cannot be fixed, then it can at least be endured. The endurance is read as commitment. Commitment is read as responsibility. The loop closes and rest becomes betrayal.

The betrayal is not explicit. No one says that resting is a failure. The person simply feels the social gravity. They notice the shift in tone if they pause. They sense the relief of others when they continue. Those signals are enough to keep the effort alive.

There is also a private betrayal. When someone has invested so much effort, stopping can feel like losing the investment. The sunk cost is emotional as well as practical. The person has built an identity on being the one who carries. To stop is to risk a loss of self.

This is why exhaustion can feel like the only proof that responsibility has been honored. The person does not trust the system to acknowledge what is invisible. So they use their own depletion as evidence. The body becomes the receipt.

This receipt is costly because it trains the person to read suffering as proof. If exhaustion is the evidence, then relief becomes suspect. The person may question whether they have earned rest, whether they have earned peace. They can become dependent on the sensation of being needed, because it confirms their role. This dependence is not chosen; it is built by repetition.

There is also a quiet sense of injustice here. The person is sacrificing for outcomes they did not fully shape. They may not name it as injustice, but the feeling registers. It is the feeling of being responsible without being respected in the way authority is respected. It is the feeling of being seen for effort and unseen for judgment.

Over time, this tension can narrow the person's emotional range. They become good at carrying, less able to imagine not carrying. The absence of authority becomes a permanent feature of their internal landscape. They adapt to it, but the adaptation is costly.

Effort can improve execution. It cannot replace authority.

No amount of diligence can compensate for the inability to decide. No amount of care can override a structure that does not permit change.

Yet effort is often deployed precisely where authority is absent, because it is the only lever available.

Authority is the right to make decisions and to allocate resources. Responsibility is the expectation that outcomes will be delivered. When those two are aligned, effort has a clear purpose. When they are separated, effort becomes a substitute for missing power. The person is held to outcomes they cannot fully control.

Responsibility flows downward by default; authority rarely follows. The person doing the work is expected to fix what they did not choose. They inherit outcomes shaped by decisions they did not make. They are held to a standard without being given the right to change the conditions.

This is where competence becomes a liability. Competence is visible and therefore recruitable. The moment a person demonstrates capability, the system adapts to use it. New tasks are routed to them not because they have agreed, but because the system has learned that the tasks get done that way.

The liability is quiet because it arrives as trust. "We know you can handle it" sounds like affirmation. But it also signals that the responsibility has already been reassigned. The person is not asked to take on the work; they are informed that the work has arrived. Their competence is treated as a resource the system can draw on without renegotiation.

This is not only in professional settings. In families, the competent child becomes the organizer. In friend groups, the capable person becomes the planner. In volunteer communities, the reliable member becomes the default coordinator. The assignment is informal, often affectionate, and rarely accompanied by formal authority to change the terms.

Authority moves slowly because it requires formal acknowledgment. Responsibility moves quickly because it only requires assumption. So responsibility continues to migrate downward, and competence accelerates the migration.

Competence also creates asymmetry. When one person can do a task faster, others become dependent on that efficiency. The system begins to allocate based on speed rather than on fairness or authority. The faster person becomes a bottleneck that no one names. They are admired for their capability and quietly relied upon for it.

Over time, this dependency can distort the distribution of learning. If one person always solves the hard parts, others do not develop the same capacity. The system becomes more lopsided. The competent person becomes more essential. Essentialness is a form of captivity.

The distortion can be emotional as well as practical. When competence is praised repeatedly, it becomes hard to disentangle identity from output. The person feels valued for what they can solve, not for who they are. That valuation makes it harder to set the work down.

The authority gap is felt most acutely when outcomes are judged. If a project fails, the person who did the work becomes the target. If a process is broken, the person who kept it running is blamed. The person is seen as the owner because they were the one present. Ownership is imputed by proximity, not granted by structure.

Authority rarely follows because authority is costly to give. To give authority is to accept risk, to change the distribution of power, to be accountable for the new distribution. Organizations and families often avoid that cost. It is easier to allow responsibility to drift downward while keeping authority stable above. The drift can be rationalized as efficiency. It is, in practice, an extraction of effort.

Sometimes the extraction is masked by the language of ownership. People are told to "own" a project or "own" a problem. The word sounds like authority, but it often means accountability without the tools to change the rules. The person is expected to deliver results, yet they must still seek approval for the decisions that would make those results possible. Ownership becomes a rhetorical transfer rather than a structural one.

This is why the experience can feel paradoxical. The person is both central and peripheral. They are central because the system relies on them. They are peripheral because the system does not grant them decision rights. They are placed at the center of responsibility while kept at the edge of authority.

The paradox intensifies when errors occur. If the outcome is bad, the person is visible and therefore accountable. If the outcome is good, the authority above can claim the success as confirmation of the existing structure. The person carries the risk without holding the power. This is a structural bargain that is rarely made explicit.

The imbalance can persist because it is relationally convenient. Authority can claim to be delegating while retaining control. The person can feel entrusted while remaining constrained. Both sides can tell a coherent story, even though the structure is misaligned. The cost is paid by the person in the middle, whose effort makes both stories seem true.

Competence makes this easier to justify. If someone is capable, it feels reasonable to rely on them. Relying becomes dependency. Dependency becomes expectation. Expectation becomes responsibility. The person is not trapped by their incompetence but by their capability.

When capability is rare, the trap deepens. The person becomes the sole translator of a domain, the only one who can interpret a complex system or navigate a specialized process. They become necessary in a way that the system does not formalize. The necessity is treated as a gift rather than as a responsibility of the system. The person is thanked for being the bridge, not granted authority over the bridge.

Authority is often preserved at the top because it is seen as the locus of accountability. But accountability without proximity is abstract. The person closest to the work is the one who feels the consequences. The one who feels the consequences becomes the one who acts. The one who acts becomes the one who is blamed if it fails. Responsibility falls to the person with proximity, while authority stays with the person with position.

Over time, this produces a subtle inversion.

Instead of asking whether the structure is wrong, the individual asks whether they are insufficient.

Instead of questioning the conditions, they question their own adequacy.

Effort becomes a way to avoid confronting limits.

The inversion is psychological and social at once. Psychologically, the person treats their own capacity as the variable under control. Socially, the group treats the person as the stabilizing agent. When a problem appears, the gaze turns toward the person who has covered it before. The issue becomes their issue.

The inversion hides the path by which responsibility migrated. Because the transfer was informal, it is hard to pinpoint. There is no moment to cite, no explicit instruction to challenge. The person simply finds themselves on the receiving end of expectation after expectation. The accumulation feels natural because it was gradual.

The identity of effort reinforces the inversion. If effort is who someone is, then questioning the structure feels like questioning the self. It becomes easier to internalize the burden than to notice the structural misalignment. The person may even feel pride in carrying it. That pride makes the trap more stable.

The inversion also protects others from discomfort. If the person blames themselves, the group does not need to confront the redistribution of authority. If the person doubts their adequacy, the system can remain unchanged. The quietness of the inversion is what allows it to persist.

The inversion also changes memory. The person remembers the moments they failed to carry everything. They forget the moments when the system failed to provide authority. Over time, their personal narrative fills with evidence of insufficiency. The structural narrative fades.

This is how a structural problem becomes a personal story. The story feels coherent. It is also incomplete. It leaves out the part where responsibility drifted while authority stayed put.

The incomplete story is not simply a misunderstanding; it is a social convenience. If the story remains personal, the solution remains personal. The person tries harder, or worries more, or doubts themselves. The structure is spared examination. The group does not have to confront the imbalance it has normalized.

Over time, the personal story can become self-reinforcing. The person finds evidence of their inadequacy in every strained outcome. They interpret each failure as proof that they must carry even more. The story becomes a lens that makes the structural problem harder to see. The more the person believes the story, the more effort they supply, and the more the structure depends on that supply.

This is why responsibility drift can persist for years without being named. The person becomes increasingly skilled at compensating. The system becomes increasingly reliant on their compensation. The reliance is mistaken for stability.

This avoidance is understandable.

Limits imply refusal. Refusal implies conflict. Conflict threatens relationships, status, or belonging.

Effort, by contrast, is safe. It is rewarded. It signals goodwill.

And so the individual keeps pushing, long after pushing stops being rational.

The safety of effort is not imaginary. In many settings, effort is the one currency that is always accepted. It can be offered without permission. It can be withdrawn only at social risk. So effort becomes the default response to ambiguity. If the role is unclear, effort fills it. If the authority is absent, effort stands in.

This is how informal expectation transfer works. No one announces the transfer; it occurs through repetition. Each time a person fills a gap, the expectation that they will fill it becomes stronger. The expectation is then assumed to be mutual, even if it was never stated. People behave as if there is an agreement. The agreement is real enough to govern behavior, yet too invisible to renegotiate.

The transfer is often cloaked in appreciation. "Thank you for handling that" sounds like closure. It can also sound like ownership. The gratitude marks the task as theirs, the way a compliment can mark a style. The next time the situation arises, the gratitude functions as memory. The memory becomes a claim on the person's attention.

This is praise as silent reassignment. The praise does not come with a formal shift in authority, but it changes the social map. It signals that the person is now associated with the outcome. If something similar happens again, the expectation follows that association. The person might even feel honored, which makes the reassignment feel voluntary. But the structure has shifted without being named.

Because the transfer is informal, it does not carry the protections of formality. There is no clear scope, no explicit resourcing, no defined endpoint. The person inherits the work but not the right to reshape it. The praise is warm; the authority is absent.

The warmth matters because it makes the transfer feel relational rather than structural. It can feel like appreciation rather than obligation. The person may accept it because refusing warmth can feel like refusing connection. So the reassignment is sealed by emotion rather than by policy.

Sometimes the transfer is framed as an opportunity. The person is told they are trusted, that this is a chance to grow, that their contribution is valued. Those frames are often sincere. They also move responsibility without moving authority. They convert a structural need into a personal narrative of growth. The person becomes the solution to a structural problem, and the structure remains unchanged.

The language of appreciation can obscure the language of obligation. When people feel grateful, they are less likely to question the terms. The person carrying the responsibility becomes reluctant to appear ungrateful. The gratitude becomes a soft lock on the role.

Informal expectations can be more binding than formal ones. Formal expectations can be negotiated, revised, or clarified. Informal expectations live in tone and history. They are enforced by subtle cues, by silence, by the slight disappointment that follows a boundary. The person feels these cues even when they are not spoken.

The drift of expectation also creates a social ledger. The person who steps in becomes the one who is "owed" gratitude. But gratitude is not authority. It does not grant the right to redirect the work or to decline it. It simply acknowledges the sacrifice. Acknowledgment can be heartfelt while still maintaining the imbalance.

Competence deepens the ledger. Each successful rescue is added to the story. The story becomes evidence that the person is the right one for the task. It is difficult for the person to contradict their own history. The past becomes a form of pressure.

There is a particular kind of fatigue that comes from this pattern.

It is not physical. It is not even emotional in the usual sense.

It is the fatigue of investing energy into a system that cannot return proportional impact.

This fatigue is confusing because it lacks a clear cause.

Nothing dramatic has happened. No single decision feels wrong.

Yet the weight accumulates.

The accumulation has a texture. It is the sense of being the last line of defense for problems that should not be personal. It is the sensation that life is spent buffering rather than building. The person becomes the shock absorber for structural misalignment. The shocks arrive anyway; they simply land on the same person each time.

Fatigue like this does not present as a single collapse. It shows up as small hesitations, a quiet dread, a background depletion that never fully recedes. It can look like burnout from the outside, but it is different in kind. Burnout often follows overwork on recognized tasks. This fatigue follows invisible work on unrecognized responsibilities.

Because the responsibilities are informal, they are hard to describe. They do not fit into a role description or a schedule. So the fatigue seems disproportionate. Others may not see it. The person may doubt it themselves. The doubt deepens the fatigue.

The pattern often persists because it remains socially functional. As long as one person continues to cover the gaps, the system does not break. The system may even appear efficient. What it is not is honest about the cost. That cost is carried in private.

Private costs are hard to translate into public arguments. The person may feel drained but cannot point to a single task that caused it. The exhaustion is distributed across dozens of small acts of compensation. Each act seems reasonable; the total is unsustainable.

Because the costs are private, they can be misread. Others may interpret the person's strain as a personal issue rather than a structural one. The person may interpret it the same way. This misreading reinforces the idea that effort is the variable to adjust. The structure remains offstage.

The private cost also includes a loss of agency. When responsibility is assumed rather than granted, the person is always reacting. They become an instrument of stability rather than an author of change. The difference is subtle but profound.

The fatigue also has a moral component. The person feels responsible for outcomes that are beyond their reach. They are praised for responsibility, so they feel it even more. The praise becomes a reminder of the expectation. This is why praise can be heavy. It is affectionate, but it is also a marker that the role has been assigned.

Over time, the fatigue can become a worldview. The person begins to assume that any responsibility will eventually become theirs, that any gap will eventually be theirs to fill. They may stop expecting structure at all. They may accept a constant state of improvisation as normal. That acceptance is a form of adaptation, but it is also a form of resignation.

The moment effort becomes a trap is not when you work hard.

It is when effort replaces the question that should have been asked earlier:

Is this something my effort can legitimately influence?

As long as that question remains unasked, effort will continue to expand— not because it is effective, but because it is available.

And availability is often mistaken for responsibility.

The question itself is not a technique. It is a signal that something in the structure is misaligned. It points to a gap between responsibility and authority, between expectation and permission. When the gap is wide, effort is asked to cross it. Effort can cross it for a while. It cannot erase it.

The trap is not the act of trying. The trap is the silent reassignment that turns trying into ownership. It is the way praise can become a contract. It is the way competence can become a claim. It is the way informal expectations can move faster than formal authority.

When responsibility migrates faster than authority, effort grows to fill the space between them. At first the growth feels like commitment. Over time it feels like obligation. Eventually it feels like exhaustion. The person has been made responsible for outcomes they do not control, and effort is the only permitted response.

The outcome is a form of captivity that looks like dedication. From the outside, it resembles reliability and care. From the inside, it feels like a role that cannot be set down. The person is not choosing the responsibility in any explicit way; the responsibility has chosen them.

This is why effort, in the absence of authority, becomes a trap. It takes the moral shape of virtue while performing the structural role of compensation. It allows a system to function without resolving its own gaps. It generates gratitude instead of change. And because the gratitude feels good and the effort feels honorable, the trap can persist indefinitely.

What persists is not only the workload but the misrecognition of what the workload means. The person is treated as unusually dedicated, when they are often simply compensating for a missing structure. Their dedication becomes a narrative that protects the structure from being questioned. The structure appears to work because someone is making it work.

The trap is thus doubly concealed. It is concealed by the person's own investment, which makes the role feel chosen. It is concealed by the group's appreciation, which makes the role feel rewarded. Both concealments are sincere. Neither resolves the underlying misalignment.

It is a trap that does not announce itself. It enters through praise, through urgency, through small acts of rescue. By the time it is felt, it has already been normalized. The person has already been positioned as the one who catches the falling responsibilities. The falling continues because it is being caught.

The migration of responsibility is therefore self-reinforcing. The more someone catches, the more the system drops. The more the system drops, the more the person catches. The loop is quiet and polite. It is also relentless. Its persistence is structural, not personal.

Effort remains the visible currency in that loop. It is what can be given without permission and taken without formal process. So it is what is asked for again and again. Authority remains where it was, insulated by the very effort that compensates for its absence. This is how responsibility migrates faster than authority, and why the person who is trying the hardest can end up with the least control.

Chapter 4

How judgment illusions are constructed

Judgment rarely feels imposed.

Most of the time, it feels earned.

That sense of earning is often attached to effort. Effort is tangible, it can be recalled, and it can be displayed. When an outcome arrives, the mind reaches for the most visible currency available, and effort is usually that currency. The translation from effort to responsibility is not logically airtight, but it is psychologically persuasive. It suggests that the result was paid for in some recognizable way, that the account was settled by the person who did the work. The structure of many environments amplifies this translation by making effort the main thing that can be tracked and talked about.

The earned feeling also draws on cultural stories about merit. We are taught, in subtle and overt ways, that results should follow from personal diligence and judgment. That teaching shapes what people expect to see, and expectation shapes what they are willing to interpret as evidence. When a situation is complex, the mind defaults to the story it already knows. The merit story is familiar and clean. It rewards effort with consequence, and it rewards clarity with plausibility. The illusion benefits from that familiarity.

Even in environments that resist simple merit stories, the earned feeling persists because it offers a boundary around responsibility. It says, implicitly, that there was a perimeter of influence, and that the person inside it used it well or poorly. That perimeter feels stable even when it is arbitrary. The feeling of earning does not require that the perimeter be accurate. It requires only that the perimeter be imaginable and that the imagined perimeter align with what others are prepared to accept.

There is a quiet satisfaction in that feeling. It gives order to experience and a sense of proportionality to consequences. It tells you that events were not random, that your choices mattered, that the world responded to the signals you put into it. Even when the outcome is painful, the idea that it was earned offers a kind of coherence. It makes the story legible, and it makes the self legible within it.

The earned feeling is reinforced by social expectation. Others treat judgment as something that should be traceable back to a person. Conversations in the aftermath of a decision assume that a recognizable chain exists between action and result. The more plausible that chain sounds, the more reasonable the judgment appears. The appearance of reasonableness is a powerful stabilizer, because it is taken as evidence even when it is only a narrative fit.

You look back at an outcome and can trace a sequence of actions: what you noticed, what you decided, what you failed to prevent.

The tracing is not usually fraudulent. It follows the traces that are visible in memory and record. It follows the lines that can be spoken out loud. It makes sense because the human mind is designed to connect events and motives. Yet visibility is not the same as completeness. A traceable sequence does not show the boundaries of what was ever possible.

The narrative appears coherent. Responsibility seems to settle naturally on your shoulders.

That settling can feel like gravity rather than a decision. It happens through small cues: the questions asked in a meeting, the way a report is written, the phrases that show up in a performance review. None of those cues needs to be explicit about blame. They simply direct attention toward the person and away from the structure. The direction is enough. Over time, that direction becomes the standard path for explanation.

The settling also benefits from the way records are created. Most organizational records are action-oriented: tickets, emails, approvals, decisions, and rejections. The record shows what someone did or did not do. It rarely shows the constraints that made certain actions meaningless or impossible. When the record becomes the basis for judgment, responsibility follows the record, not the unrecorded boundary.

A coherent narrative is also easier to carry forward. It can be repeated without qualification, which makes it stable across audiences. The stability itself becomes a sign of truth. People trust what they can repeat. The ability to repeat a story without caveats is not evidence of accuracy, but it is treated as such because it enables organizational memory to function without constantly reopening questions.

Coherence has a gravitational pull. Once a narrative has settled into a clean line, it becomes uncomfortable to disturb. Ambiguity looks like evasion. Complexity looks like excuse. This is not because people are foolish. It is because the structure of accountability is built on clarity, not on accuracy. Clarity is cheaper to maintain than accuracy.

There is also a subtle emotional relief in a single line of responsibility. If you can identify where things went wrong, the situation feels less chaotic. The line becomes a substitute for control, even if no control existed at the time. In that way, judgment can offer comfort even as it distorts.

This is not an accident.

It is an artifact of design choices that prioritize coordination over comprehension. Systems need to act. They need to close questions and move forward. The cost of keeping every structural uncertainty visible is high, and it slows the pace of judgment. So the system simplifies. The simplification is not necessarily cynical; it is operational.

But operational simplification shapes perception, and perception is the raw material of judgment.

The same operational pressure appears in personal narratives. People want to know where they stand. They want a stable account of what happened and what it means. The mind settles on a story that can support that stability. The story is not fabricated; it is compressed. Compression leaves out the invisible constraints, and the result is an illusion that feels like clarity.

Judgment illusions are not created by deception. They are created by structure.

Structure is a kind of background decision-making that survives its makers. Once in place, it continues to shape what is noticed and what is ignored, even when the people involved have changed. The illusion is therefore stable across time. It does not depend on any one person believing a false story. It depends on repeated exposure to the same selective visibility.

This is why misjudgment can appear in environments full of competent, sincere people. The illusion does not require ignorance. It requires ordinary participation in a system that filters reality. A person can be attentive, ethical, and diligent, and still be guided toward a conclusion that feels reasonable but is structurally incomplete.

The manufacturing happens through repetition. Each cycle of evaluation reproduces the same emphasis on visible action and the same silence around constraint. Each cycle trains the next. Over time, the pattern becomes indistinguishable from common sense. The illusion is not a moment of confusion; it is a stable state produced by the architecture of work.

Structures do not have to be malicious to be distorting. They can be efficient, stable, or well intentioned and still manufacture illusion. The point is not that someone lied. The point is that the system decides what can be seen, what can be said, and what is treated as real. When those decisions are embedded in routine, the resulting misjudgment feels like ordinary truth.

A structure is a pattern that repeats without being argued each time. It can be a workflow, a role design, a reporting chain, a budgeting cycle, or a set of informal expectations. Once it repeats, it begins to feel like the world itself, not a choice. Judgment then takes the shape of that world. People learn to evaluate within it, not outside it.

Specifically, by structures that expose execution while concealing control.

Control is often treated as a private matter. It is negotiated in rooms where the record is thin, it is embedded in budgets that look neutral, and it is exercised through informal signals that are easy to miss. Execution, in contrast, happens in public. It creates artifacts that can be audited and compared. This difference ensures that responsibility settles on the visible layer, not the controlling layer.

The concealment is rarely absolute. It is partial and diffuse. Pieces of control are visible to different people at different moments. No single person sees the whole map. As a result, the map is treated as if it does not exist. When people cannot collectively point to the structure, they default to the evidence they share, and that evidence is usually about what was done, not what was permitted.

Control is also temporal. Decisions that set conditions can happen long before the moment of execution. By the time the outcome is judged, those earlier decisions have faded, and the people who made them may not be present. The temporal gap turns a controlling decision into a background fact, and background facts are rarely treated as objects of judgment.

Execution leaves footprints. It creates artifacts, timestamps, conversations, tasks completed and tasks missed. Control, in contrast, is often exercised upstream, quietly, and without visible residue. Control is in the decision about which problems are allowed to exist, which constraints are treated as fixed, and which tradeoffs are considered legitimate. Those decisions rarely leave a trace that is read as evidence.

You see what you did. You do not see what you were never allowed to decide.

The asymmetry can be mundane. A team may be told to deliver an outcome on a timeline that was negotiated elsewhere. A manager may be held responsible for morale inside a culture they did not set. A professional may be expected to prevent risks that were accepted by someone else months earlier. The actions are public. The constraints are private. Judgment follows the visible layer.

Over time, the visible layer becomes mistaken for the whole system.

This mistake is trained. New members of a system are taught how to read the visible layer because that is what is available. They learn the rituals of status updates, the cadence of deadlines, the language of accountability. They do not learn the hidden negotiations that set the stage, because those are not part of the official curriculum. The result is a learned blindness that looks like competence.

The visible layer is also where reassurance lives. If everything important is visible, then everything important is manageable. The system benefits from the appearance of manageability. It reduces anxiety and makes coordination feel possible. The cost is that judgment begins from an incomplete picture and rarely admits that incompleteness.

This mistake becomes self-reinforcing. The more the visible layer is treated as the whole, the more the invisible layer is ignored. The ignored layer becomes less discussed, less documented, and less likely to be remembered. That absence then appears as proof that it did not matter. The illusion deepens without anyone having to add more deception.

Environmental distortion plays a large role in this process. The environment of judgment is not just physical but informational. It is the set of signals that are amplified, the time horizons that are privileged, and the data that is considered legitimate. If the environment highlights responsiveness and downplays constraint, then the environment is already steering judgment before any individual draws a conclusion.

The distortion is structural because it is built into how attention is organized. Some information is available only to certain roles, or only at certain times, or only in certain formats. A dashboard can turn a complex situation into a simple green light. A meeting agenda can make a binding decision feel like an offhand remark. These are not acts of deception. They are ordinary designs of attention.

Even the physical arrangement of work can distort judgment. Proximity to decision makers can make authority feel larger than it is, while distance can make authority feel absent. Open-plan visibility can make execution look like constant agency, while private negotiation rooms hide the contours of real control. The environment trains the body to notice certain cues and ignore others, and those trained perceptions shape judgment later on.

Digital systems add their own distortions. Metrics travel faster than context. A single number can summarize months of constraint, and the number will be treated as the primary truth because it is portable. The portability of metrics makes them persuasive in evaluation. What is not portable falls away. This is not a flaw of the metric itself; it is the consequence of building judgment on what travels easily.

Consider how evaluation typically works.

Evaluation tends to aggregate. It compresses months of work into a handful of ratings, a small set of narratives, or a limited group of decisive incidents. Compression is necessary for administrative reasons, but it privileges certain kinds of evidence. Incidents with clear actions and clear outcomes become the center of attention. Long-term constraints, slow accumulations, and structural bottlenecks are less likely to be condensed into a single evaluative phrase.

Evaluation is also shaped by the need to compare. Comparisons require a shared scale, and shared scales rarely include the hidden constraints unique to each role or moment. As a result, evaluation emphasizes behaviors that are easily comparable: speed, responsiveness, visibility, and apparent initiative. The comparability requirement pushes structural nuance to the margins.

The social context of evaluation matters as well. Evaluations are often delivered in a tone of fairness and professional care. That tone makes the judgment feel considered and balanced. Yet a tone can mask the underlying asymmetry of information. The evaluators may be just as constrained as the evaluated, relying on the visible layer because that is what they can access. The illusion is then reproduced not out of malice but out of practical limitation.

In many environments, evaluation is retrospective, formalized, and tied to visible behaviors. It occurs after a project, after a failure, after a review cycle. It relies on artifacts that can be read and scored. The evaluation is not only about what was done but about what can be seen to have been done. That distinction matters because it ensures that visibility is treated as value.

You are assessed on responsiveness. On initiative. On how well you anticipate problems.

Those criteria are not arbitrary. They reflect an ideal of personal agency and forward-looking competence. They also fit neatly into the kinds of evidence organizations can collect. Responsiveness can be measured by time stamps and replies. Initiative can be inferred from proposals and tasks started. Anticipation can be inferred from risks surfaced. The criteria match the evidence, and the evidence is the surface layer.

Visibility can become a performance requirement. People learn to narrate their own actions in a way that aligns with the criteria, not necessarily because they are deceptive, but because that is how they are understood. The result is a subtle shift in attention: effort is directed toward actions that produce recognizable signals, while actions that would address structural constraints but leave little visible trace are deprioritized. The environment makes one kind of work legible and another kind of work easy to miss.

This legibility gap does not stay external. It becomes a self-assessment gap. Individuals begin to evaluate their own performance based on the same visible criteria, not because those criteria are inherently wrong, but because they are the only ones consistently rewarded. Over time, the criteria shape identity, and identity shapes judgment. The illusion is thus maintained from both outside and inside.

What they do not evaluate is whether you had legitimate authority to shape the conditions in which those problems arose.

Authority is hard to measure because it is not always formal. It can be partial, delegated, or negotiated. It can be constrained by budget, by policy, by leadership mood, or by hidden dependencies. It can be conditional on political capital that is never recorded. The result is that authority is treated as a given when it is actually a variable. Judgment then assumes a level of control that may never have existed.

When authority is treated as a given, the evaluation process collapses context into character. Decisions appear to reflect personal judgment rather than structural permission. This collapse makes evaluation feel fair because it uses a single yardstick. It also makes evaluation inaccurate because it ignores the uneven terrain on which that yardstick is applied. The effect is subtle: people can disagree about the severity of a judgment while still accepting the underlying illusion that control was available.

Authority can also be situational, shifting with timing and political attention. In a moment of crisis, a person may have latitude that disappears a week later. In a moment of calm, the same person may be tightly bound by procedure. Evaluations rarely capture that temporal variability. They flatten authority into a stable trait, and that flattening feeds the illusion that the person could have decided differently in any moment.

These distortions are not merely administrative. They shape how individuals are expected to feel about their own actions. If the system treats authority as stable, then the individual is encouraged to treat responsibility as stable as well. The resulting self-judgment can become severe, because it is anchored in an assumption the system never fully examined.

This omission is subtle, but decisive.

It changes the baseline of evaluation. If it is assumed that you could have shaped the conditions, then any failure inside those conditions becomes yours. The omission converts a structural limitation into a personal deficit. It does so without the appearance of unfairness, because the limitation was never made legible enough to be debated.

Incentive-driven misreading thrives in this setting. People are rewarded for appearing to have agency, for projecting control, and for speaking the language of ownership. Admitting to structural limits can read as weakness or deflection. The incentives are not always explicit. They are embedded in who is promoted, whose ideas are taken seriously, and who is invited into the next circle of decision. The misreading is not a mistake; it is an adaptation to the reward structure.

The adaptation shapes the stories people tell about outcomes. It becomes safer to interpret a failure as a lapse of judgment than as a consequence of misaligned authority. The first interpretation is actionable within the system, while the second points to structural change that may be politically expensive. By choosing the safer interpretation, the environment preserves itself. The illusion is not only a cognitive error; it is a survival strategy within a particular set of incentives.

The illusion forms when feedback is asymmetric.

Feedback systems are designed to detect deviations in action, not deviations in authority. They are built around what can be observed and measured. Logs, tickets, alerts, and performance indicators all record actions and outputs. Very few record the absence of permission. When the system does not track a constraint, the constraint becomes socially weightless. It exists in private understanding but not in institutional memory.

Asymmetry is thus reinforced by instrumentation. What is instrumented becomes real; what is not instrumented becomes questionable. The choice of what to instrument is a structural decision that predates any particular judgment. Yet it shapes every judgment that follows by defining what counts as evidence. The illusion is built into the architecture of evidence, not merely into the opinions of individuals.

Asymmetry is not only about volume of feedback but about what feedback is about. Action generates responses because actions are visible and often measurable. Constraints, however, are often invisible and thus do not trigger correction signals. The feedback system therefore trains attention toward actions and away from conditions. Over time, that training begins to feel like a property of reality.

Actions generate feedback. Constraints do not.

The absence of feedback on constraints is easily misunderstood. It can look like neutrality or irrelevance. It can also look like acceptance, as if the conditions were settled by collective agreement rather than by inaccessible decisions. The silence around constraints becomes a subtle endorsement of them, making them seem natural rather than constructed.

You receive signals about what you did wrong, but silence about what you could never have done right.

The silence has a psychological effect. It tempts the mind to fill the gap with imagined possibility. If no one said the constraint was binding, perhaps it was not. If no one told you the boundary existed, perhaps it could have been crossed. The absence of explicit constraint becomes an invitation to blame, even when the constraint was real and durable.

Silence is easily misread as absence rather than exclusion.

This is one way normalized false conclusions are formed. If the environment treats the lack of discussion as the lack of importance, then conclusions are drawn without the missing data. Over time, the false conclusions are not experienced as false. They are experienced as common sense. The misjudgment becomes part of the normal vocabulary of evaluation.

The asymmetry also shapes self-perception. When the only feedback you receive is about your actions, you begin to treat action as the primary lever available to you. That internal model makes the constraint layer recede even further. The result is a self-reinforcing illusion that feels like realism because it is supported by all the available signals.

The illusion is strengthened by the ordinary rhythm of work. When tasks arrive continuously, the immediate demand is to respond, not to analyze the origin of the demand. The rhythm creates a bias toward action and away from structural reflection. Over time, this bias is experienced as professionalism. The person who pauses to question the boundary can be seen as slowing the work, while the person who acts is seen as dependable. The asymmetry thus becomes a social norm.

Once a social norm is in place, disagreement with the norm appears risky. The risk does not have to be overt. It can be as simple as being perceived as uncooperative. That subtle risk is enough to make most people accept the action-centered frame. The illusion persists not because people are unaware, but because the cost of challenging it feels higher than the cost of accepting it.

Another ingredient is temporal distance.

Temporal distance allows the record to be curated. People gather notes, assemble timelines, and select which artifacts will stand as evidence. The curation is usually honest, but it is not neutral. It privileges what was preserved and what can be summarized. Moments of ambiguity and conflict often leave weaker traces than moments of decisive action. The curated record thus favors the appearance of decision over the reality of uncertainty.

Distance also changes who participates in the narrative. Those who were closest to the constraints may have moved on, while those who remain interpret the past through the lens of current priorities. The story becomes less about what it felt like in the moment and more about what the organization needs to believe about itself now. The shift is subtle, but it changes the way judgment is framed.

As time passes, the emotional intensity of the original moment fades. Without that intensity, it becomes difficult to recall why certain options felt impossible. The mind remembers the sequence but not the pressure. That loss of pressure makes the alternatives look more available than they were. Judgment then treats the past as if it were calm, even when it was not.

Time changes the texture of memory. In the moment, uncertainty is vivid, competing pressures are sharp, and options are ambiguous. Later, those sensations are muted. What remains is a simplified record. The record is not necessarily wrong, but it is thinner, and thinner records yield narrower judgments.

Judgment is often applied after outcomes materialize. By then, the original uncertainty has collapsed into a single narrative.

The collapse is partly emotional. The mind wants to settle. It wants to know what happened. It wants to stabilize the story so that the future feels predictable. The settling turns a field of possibilities into a linear story of cause and effect. When that story becomes the basis for judgment, the uncertainty that shaped the original decision disappears from view.

Alternative paths disappear. Unchosen options fade.

The fading is not neutral. Options that were never fully available fade just as quickly as those that were. That creates the impression that everything was once possible and merely left unchosen. The disappearance of the boundary between possible and impossible is a core mechanism of illusion.

What remains is a clean line from action to result.

The line is simple enough to explain, and simple enough to assign. It offers a tidy allocation of responsibility. It also hides the dynamic nature of the moment, in which signals were partial, timing was constrained, and incentives were mixed. The line is a product of time as much as it is a product of evidence.

This retrospective clarity is seductive.

It feels like truth because it is coherent. But coherence can be a property of narrative, not of reality. The seduction is that clarity becomes equated with accuracy, and once that equation is accepted, the judgment feels inevitable.

Organizations often reinforce this seduction through rituals of closure. Postmortems, reviews, and summaries are designed to reach a clear conclusion. The conclusion is expected to be teachable and actionable, which pushes it toward individual choices rather than structural constraints. A conclusion that says "the system made this likely" is harder to translate into a single action, so it is less likely to be chosen as the official story. The ritual therefore favors the illusion, even when participants are aware of the limits.

The same dynamic appears in personal memory. People prefer to end a difficult episode with a clean lesson, and the cleanest lessons are about individual decisions. The lesson is satisfying because it implies future control. It is also misleading because it ignores the structural forces that made the outcome likely in the first place. The seduction of clarity thus works at both institutional and personal levels.

In hindsight, everything looks decidable.

The decision space is flattened into a set of choices that appear obvious. That appearance is a consequence of learning the outcome.

When the outcome is known, signals that pointed in that direction are remembered and signals that pointed elsewhere are ignored. The mind reconstructs the decision moment as if the path had always been visible. It rarely was.

Hindsight also changes the meaning of ordinary cues. A small warning sign can be reinterpreted as a clear signal, and a routine delay can be reinterpreted as a decisive turning point. The reinterpretation is not necessarily dishonest; it is an attempt to align the past with the present. But alignment is not the same as accuracy. It creates the impression that the decision should have been easy.

The flattening affects how others view the decision maker. A complex judgment becomes a simple mistake. The person is evaluated not on the difficulty of the moment, but on the simplicity of the narrative. That evaluation feels fair because the narrative feels clear. The clarity hides the ways in which the moment was actually complex and contested.

You should have known. You should have acted earlier. You should have pushed harder.

These phrases are ubiquitous because they sound reasonable. They suggest that the outcome was latent and that the right person would have recognized it. Yet the reasonableness is often a function of outcome knowledge, not of the information available at the time. The phrases perform moral work by locating a failure in a person rather than in a structure.

The system retroactively assigns competence to a moment that never had it.

This assignment is not always malicious. It is often a byproduct of storytelling. But it has consequences. It transforms ordinary uncertainty into a personal deficit. It also magnifies the expectation of control. The retroactive assignment makes the system look more coherent and the individual look more culpable.

Retroactive competence is appealing because it suggests that good judgment is a stable trait. If competence could have saved the situation, then competence becomes the solution, and the system can continue without altering its structure. The illusion thus protects the system from the need to examine its own design. It keeps the focus on the individual's capacity rather than on the environment that constrained that capacity.

This logic also shapes how success is interpreted. When an outcome is positive, competence is assigned retroactively as well. Success becomes proof that the person had control, even if the outcome was driven by factors outside their authority. The person is praised, the system is affirmed, and the structural context is ignored. The same illusion that produces blame also produces misplaced credit.

Temporal distance makes incentive-driven misreading more plausible. After the fact, it is easier for a system to protect itself by framing the outcome as a failure of individual judgment rather than as a failure of design. The distance reduces the risk of contradiction, because fewer people remember the original constraints with precision. The misreading becomes safer to deploy.

Language plays a quiet role here.

Language is not neutral. It encodes assumptions about agency, capability, and intention. The grammatical forms used in evaluation subtly declare who had options and who did not. When language presumes agency, it turns structural limits into personal shortcomings without having to say so explicitly.

Labels such as "owner," "driver," and "accountable" sound descriptive, but they are also prescriptive. They assign a kind of moral weight that exceeds formal authority. Once a label is applied, it is difficult to argue that the labeled person lacked control, because the label itself implies control. Language does not simply report reality; it establishes a default interpretation of it.

Phrases like "you could have raised it," "you should have escalated," or "why didn't you stop this" imply that the option was real.

The implication does not have to be argued. The phrase does the work. It establishes a norm of action and then judges the absence of that action. It also makes the absence feel willful, even when it was constrained. The power of these phrases is that they turn an invisible boundary into a visible lapse.

But implication is not evidence.

An option can be theoretically imaginable and practically unavailable at the same time.

The difference between imaginable and available is rarely noted in formal judgment. It is more convenient to treat imagination as possibility because it keeps responsibility localized. The language makes the possible look practical and the practical look chosen. It is a subtle shift, but it is one that repeatedly produces the illusion of personal failure.

Language also normalizes false conclusions by repetition. When a phrase becomes standard in post-event discussions, it frames the event in a stable way. The framing hardens into a template that can be reused. Over time, the template becomes the default explanation, even if it does not fit the specific realities of each case. The normalization is not explicit; it is embedded in how people talk.

The normalization also shapes what questions are considered reasonable. Once a phrase becomes standard, alternative framings feel eccentric or confrontational. The conversation stays within the bounds set by the standard language. Those bounds typically favor interpretations that emphasize personal control and de-emphasize structural constraint. The illusion is therefore sustained not only by what is said, but by what is made hard to say.

Judgment illusions persist because they align with moral intuitions.

Most people want a world in which actions matter and consequences follow. The desire is not naïve; it is part of how social trust is maintained. Without some belief in agency, accountability becomes empty. But the same desire makes it easy to accept judgments that are structurally distorted, because the judgments satisfy a moral preference for causality.

Moral intuition also tends to personalize harm. When a bad outcome occurs, the immediate impulse is to ask who allowed it. That impulse is useful in many contexts, but it can override structural analysis. The question "who" arrives before the question "how," and the answer to "who" often feels sufficient. The illusion gains stability because it satisfies the moral impulse quickly.

We want outcomes to be attributable. We prefer agency to ambiguity. Blame feels cleaner than structural opacity.

Ambiguity creates discomfort. It suggests that no one was in charge, that the system may have drifted, or that the event was a product of diffuse constraints. Those are unsettling possibilities. Assigning judgment to a person feels more stable. It provides a focal point for explanation and a target for moral evaluation.

Assigning judgment to an individual restores order to the story.

Even when it distorts reality.

This restoration is culturally reinforced. Institutions often celebrate decisive agency and punish acknowledgment of structural limits. Narratives of heroism and failure are built around individuals rather than systems. The structure of praise mirrors the structure of blame. In both directions, the system is obscured.

Public accountability rituals deepen this pattern. A single person apologizing or being corrected signals that the system has resolved the issue. The ritual has social value because it closes the loop. But it also conceals the continuing structural conditions that produced the outcome. The closure feels morally satisfying, which makes the illusion hard to dislodge.

The alignment with moral intuitions also makes the illusion resilient. If a judgment feels morally satisfying, challenges to it can be perceived as excuses rather than as corrections. The social cost of disrupting the narrative keeps the narrative stable. The illusion persists because it fits the emotional economy of accountability.

The most durable illusions are the ones we participate in ourselves.

Self-judgment has its own force. It is not merely a reaction to external blame. It is often a proactive effort to make sense of a situation and to retain a sense of agency. By replaying the past, the mind tries to preserve the idea that outcomes can be shaped. That preservation can be psychologically protective, yet it deepens the illusion.

Participation is reinforced by identity. Many people define themselves by their capacity to manage complexity. When a situation goes wrong, the internal response is not only about what happened but about who one is. The illusion becomes a way to protect identity: if the outcome could have been different, then competence still matters. The belief is comforting, but it also anchors responsibility in the self rather than in the system.

Professional cultures intensify this dynamic. They celebrate mastery and decisiveness. They teach people to take ownership even when ownership is partial. The culture does not necessarily demand that individuals claim full control, but it rewards those who do. The result is a subtle pressure to interpret structural limits as personal challenges rather than as binding constraints.

You replay events. You locate points of hesitation. You imagine alternative moves.

The replay offers a feeling of improvement, even if no improvement was possible. It creates the impression that the past contained hidden levers that were simply missed. The imagined levers become a form of self-discipline: a way of saying that a better version of you would have found the right move. The illusion is reinforced because the alternative version feels morally appealing.

This internal replay creates the sense that the situation was navigable, that a better version of you could have steered it differently.

The illusion is personalized.

Personalization makes it hard to distinguish between learning and self-blame. It can feel like insight when it is actually a narrowing of the frame. The person becomes the site of correction, rather than the system. That focus can seem virtuous, yet it obscures the structural production of misjudgment.

Personalization also changes how future events are interpreted. When the self is the presumed site of correction, new situations are filtered through the expectation of personal control. This can create a persistent sense of vigilance, as if every variable can and should be managed. The vigilance is exhausting, but it feels responsible. The structure that created the vigilance remains unchallenged because the focus stays on the individual.

Incentive-driven misreading can become internalized. If career progression rewards the language of ownership, individuals may adopt that language privately as well. They learn to narrate their own experiences in terms of personal responsibility because that is the currency of recognition. The internal narrative and the external incentives converge.

What goes unexamined is whether the system would have responded differently at all.

Systems have inertia. They continue in a direction unless strong counterforces intervene. Many environments are designed to resist disruption, not because of malice but because stability is valued. When judgment assumes that a different action would have changed the outcome, it often ignores the inertia that would have absorbed that action.

Inertia is reinforced by dependencies. When multiple groups depend on a particular arrangement, even a recognized flaw can be difficult to change. The cost of altering the arrangement is distributed unevenly, which makes it politically risky. A person operating within that structure may have little ability to change it, yet later judgment may assume that change was available. The illusion is fed by the hindsight belief that the system could have pivoted quickly if only someone had acted decisively.

The belief in easy pivots is itself a structural narrative. It serves to maintain confidence in the system's flexibility. If the system is believed to be flexible, then failures can be attributed to lack of will rather than to limits of design. This belief protects the system's legitimacy, but it distorts the reality of what was possible.

Whether escalation had teeth. Whether objections carried weight. Whether refusal was possible without disproportionate cost.

These questions are not always asked because they feel abstract or because they implicate higher levels of authority. Yet they are concrete in their effects. If escalation does not alter priorities, then escalation is symbolic. If objections are heard but not acted on, then objection is performative. If refusal results in punishment, then refusal was never truly on the table. These conditions are real, but they can be kept quiet by the structure of evaluation.

These questions feel abstract, so they are skipped.

Skipping them is itself a structural habit. It keeps the evaluation manageable and keeps responsibility localized. It also protects the legitimacy of the system by avoiding inquiry into how decisions are actually made. The resulting judgment appears focused and disciplined, yet it rests on an intentional narrowing of the frame.

Environmental distortion deepens the skipping. If the environment highlights individual choices but obscures institutional responses, then the questions about system response feel like speculation rather than evidence. The environment thus shapes what counts as a reasonable question. The distortion is built into the availability of data, the accessibility of records, and the social acceptability of raising certain issues.

The social acceptability piece is quiet but powerful. Asking about system response can be interpreted as questioning leadership or exposing fragility. In some environments, that interpretation carries cost. People learn to avoid the question not because they lack curiosity, but because they understand the social terrain. The result is a self-censoring dynamic that further reduces the visibility of structural limits.

Judgment illusions thrive in environments where responsibility is emphasized but authority is diffused.

Diffused authority can be a design choice. It can protect against unilateral decisions, distribute risk, or encourage collaboration. But diffusion also makes it harder to locate control. When authority is dispersed across committees, stakeholders, or informal coalitions, it becomes difficult to say who could have changed what. Judgment then attaches to the person whose actions are most visible.

Complex supply chains and regulated environments amplify this dynamic. Decisions are split across legal, compliance, operations, and external partners. Each group holds a piece of the decision, but no single group controls the outcome. When something goes wrong, the system searches for a clear line of responsibility and often finds only the most visible actor. The structural diffusion is real, but it is not rewarded with structural judgment.

Where outcomes are collective, but accountability is individual.

This mismatch is common. Projects are often delivered by teams, yet performance reviews are individual. Outcomes are the product of interdependent work, yet the language of evaluation is personal. The mismatch is not necessarily a mistake; it may be a function of administrative convenience. But it produces a structural bias toward individual blame.

Where decision rights are informal, yet consequences are formal.

Informal decision rights are hard to document. They depend on relationships, timing, and perceived influence. Formal consequences, however, are recorded and enforceable. The difference between the informal and the formal means that a person can be judged against a set of expectations that were never explicit and never fully attainable.

In such environments, judgment feels unavoidable.

It feels unavoidable because the environment does not provide a stable alternative. There is no clear structure for attributing systemic responsibility, so individual responsibility becomes the default. The default is not a decision made anew each time; it is a habit built into the structure of the organization and the language of evaluation.

Normalized false conclusions become institutional memory. Once an environment repeatedly attributes outcomes to individual judgment, that attribution becomes the expected explanation. New events are interpreted through the same lens. The institution remembers the person and forgets the structure. This is how illusions are manufactured not once but repeatedly.

The repetition has a cumulative effect. Each time a judgment is framed as personal, the system gains confidence in that framing. The framing becomes part of training, part of the implicit code of conduct, part of the stories that circulate as warnings. Newcomers inherit a narrative in which responsibility is personal by default. The illusion becomes a tradition.

Once established, the illusion reinforces itself.

A person who internalizes responsibility behaves differently. They take on more than their share, not because they are instructed to, but because the internal narrative tells them it is necessary. That behavior then appears to validate the narrative. The system sees a person taking ownership and concludes that ownership was available all along.

The reinforcement also affects who stays and who leaves. Those who accept the personal-responsibility frame are more likely to persist and be rewarded. Those who resist it may disengage or exit. Over time, the environment becomes populated by people who have already internalized the illusion, which makes the illusion feel even more natural. The structure selects for the narrative that supports it.

You take ownership to compensate. You work harder to prevent recurrence. You internalize vigilance as a virtue.

The compensatory behavior creates visible effort, which then becomes the evidence that effort is the right unit of accountability. The system reacts to what it can see and then uses what it sees to justify its judgment. The loop is tight and difficult to break because each iteration produces more of the same kind of evidence.

From the outside, this looks like maturity. From the inside, it feels like burden.

The difference between these perspectives matters. The external view treats the burden as a sign of character. The internal view experiences it as a sign of structural mismatch. Both can be true at once, and that ambiguity is part of why the illusion persists. The system reads maturity, the individual feels weight, and the structure remains unchanged.

Incentive-driven misreading is embedded in this reinforcement. Those who accept the burden are often rewarded. Those who question the legitimacy of the burden are often sidelined. The incentives align with the illusion, ensuring that it continues to replicate itself.

The reinforcement is not only economic or professional. It is social. People who accept the burden are seen as reliable and are trusted with more responsibility. That trust becomes another form of evidence that the original responsibility was legitimate. The system reads the willingness to carry weight as proof that the weight belonged there. The illusion is thus anchored in social recognition as well as formal reward.

The illusion does not collapse easily.

It does not break when you learn more. It does not break when you become more skilled.

Knowledge can sharpen the sense of responsibility rather than dissolve it. The more you understand the mechanics of a system, the more you can imagine hypothetical interventions. The imagination can outpace actual authority. The result is a form of expertise that increases the sense of personal obligation without increasing control.

New information often gets assimilated into the existing frame. If the frame says the individual was responsible, then new facts are interpreted in a way that preserves that responsibility. Facts that point to structural constraint are treated as context rather than as determinants. The illusion is flexible enough to absorb evidence without changing its core assumption.

There is also a moral risk in abandoning the illusion. If the illusion is removed, then many past judgments are called into question. The cost of that reevaluation can feel too high. The system avoids the cost by maintaining the illusion. Individuals do the same because the alternative can feel like surrendering agency. The illusion thus persists as a moral compromise.

In fact, competence often deepens it.

Competence brings confidence and heightened awareness of what might have been done. It also increases expectations from others. People assume that a competent person could have navigated constraints more effectively. The competent person may begin to accept that assumption, even when the constraints were immovable.

Competence also makes it easier to see potential leverage points, and seeing potential leverage points makes it harder to accept that they were not usable. The mind treats visibility of a lever as proof that the lever could have been pulled. This is another instance of imagined possibility being mistaken for available authority. The more skilled the person, the more levers they can imagine, and the stronger the illusion becomes.

The more capable you are, the easier it becomes to imagine that you should have been able to do more.

The imagination becomes a trap. It expands the sense of responsibility while the structural limits remain fixed. The gap between imagined control and actual control becomes a source of self-judgment. The illusion thus grows stronger as capability grows.

This dynamic is especially potent in environments that celebrate expertise. The culture expects that expertise can overcome obstacles, even when those obstacles are political, economic, or institutional. The expectation is flattering but unrealistic. It fosters a form of misjudgment that is difficult to detect because it is cloaked in praise.

The praise also has a temporal effect. A person who has been successful in the past may be expected to replicate success in a new environment, even if the structural conditions are different. Past competence is projected forward as if it were portable across constraints. When the projection fails, the failure is read as a lapse rather than as a mismatch between capability and structure. The illusion thus converts a change in conditions into a judgment about the person.

Judgment illusions are powerful because they feel reasonable.

They rarely announce themselves as false. They simply narrow the frame until responsibility fits.

The narrowing is accomplished by structure, by incentive, by time, by language, and by moral intuition. Each element alone might be manageable, but together they create a stable apparatus of misjudgment. The apparatus does not need to be designed. It emerges from ordinary practices that feel practical and efficient.

Reasonableness is a social currency. People rely on it to decide whom to trust and which explanations to accept. An explanation that feels reasonable is often accepted without further investigation, especially when the investigation would be difficult or costly. The illusion leverages this reliance. It offers a reasonable story that aligns with the evidence that is easiest to access.

The reasonableness also reduces conflict. If a judgment sounds reasonable, then disagreement can be framed as defensiveness rather than as a legitimate challenge. The illusion thus gains social protection. It is not merely a mistaken idea; it is an idea that keeps conversations smooth. That smoothness is valuable in organizations, and it incentivizes the acceptance of reasonable stories even when they are incomplete.

And once responsibility fits, the question of legitimacy quietly disappears.

The disappearance is quiet because the judgment already feels complete. To ask about legitimacy would introduce ambiguity, and ambiguity is costly. The system prefers to move forward with a clear allocation of blame or credit. The clarity becomes the operational truth, even when it is not the structural truth.

What remains is the everyday experience of carrying judgment that feels personal but is manufactured. The illusion is not a mask that can simply be removed. It is a way of seeing that has been trained by the environment. It persists not because people are unaware, but because the structure makes the illusion look like the only available account.

The cost of reopening legitimacy is often reputational. Questioning a settled judgment can be interpreted as undermining trust or avoiding accountability. That interpretation discourages deeper inquiry. The system therefore treats the settled judgment as a boundary, not a hypothesis. Once a boundary is set, it is rarely revisited, and the illusion becomes durable by default.

When judgment feels earned, it is easy to forget that the structure taught you what to count as evidence. It is easy to forget that the environment edited the record before you ever began to evaluate it. The illusion is powerful because it is quiet, normal, and endlessly repeated. It turns the architecture of constraint into the psychology of responsibility.

Chapter 5

Feedback Loops That Never Close

Some systems survive by keeping feedback incomplete.

They do not survive because they are efficient, or because they are accurate, or because they are just. They survive because the loop that would prove them wrong never quite closes.

A closed loop is a simple promise: action produces information, and the information returns to change the action. It is the idea that reality gets a vote. When the loop closes, the system has to feel the consequences of what it did. When the loop never closes, the system can continue without being forced to change.

The most familiar version of incompleteness is delay. Consequences do arrive, but later, after attention has moved on, after the record is blurred, after the people who chose the path are no longer the ones standing at the end of it. Delay creates the appearance of progress while deferring the cost of proof.

A slow loop is not necessarily broken. It can still produce feedback. But a slow loop is easy to ignore, and easy to interpret. In the space between action and consequence, stories grow. The story fills the gap before the facts do.

When feedback is delayed long enough, the system learns a new rhythm. Decisions are made in the present, justification is written later, and the future is asked to be polite about what it finds. The gap becomes a place where responsibility can be relocated, softened, or erased.

Another form of incompleteness is partial confirmation. The loop closes just enough to reassure, but not enough to settle. A small signal arrives and is treated as a verdict, even though it is only a hint. The system receives a whisper and calls it a witness.

Partial confirmation is persuasive because it feels like evidence. It is the early result that points in the desired direction. It is the narrow success that stands in for the whole picture. It is the brief moment when the model seems to work, and no one wants to disturb it with a larger test.

The third form is perpetual anticipation. The loop is framed as about to close, always about to close. The evidence is on its way, the review is scheduled, the update is imminent. The future is kept as a promise rather than a record.

Anticipation is not empty hope. It is a tool. When a system can hold people in the state of waiting, it keeps them participating without having to prove itself. Waiting becomes part of the structure, not a temporary inconvenience.

These three forms of incompleteness can coexist. The system delays the heavy feedback, accepts a light confirmation, and extends an invitation to keep waiting. Together, they create a loop that feels responsive but never delivers finality.

Entrapment deepens in that space. The person inside the loop does not feel ignored. They feel engaged. They are receiving signals, being asked for updates, attending briefings, contributing effort. It feels like movement even when it is only circulation.

The texture of an incomplete loop is subtle. It is not a single lie. It is a series of small, plausible explanations. Each one makes sense on its own. Together, they turn uncertainty into a stable environment.

The loop never closes, but it does not obviously fail. Failure would be a kind of closure. Failure would have an edge to it. In an incomplete loop, the edge is softened, rounded off by distance and interpretation.

There is a temptation to think that such systems are merely dysfunctional. But incompleteness can be functional. It can keep an organization together, or keep a project funded, or keep a relationship stable, precisely because it does not force a confrontation with reality.

In a bureaucratic system, delay can be formal. There are timelines, review periods, buffers, escalation paths. Each one seems reasonable. Each one can be justified as caution. Taken together, they ensure that the most consequential feedback arrives after the moment when it could have changed the decision.

In a market system, delay can be financial. Costs are absorbed in the long term, while revenue is counted in the short term. The quarterly report closes quickly. The larger ecological or social consequences arrive on a different calendar, sometimes on a different balance sheet.

In a personal system, delay is psychological. Regret has a long fuse. By the time it detonates, it is already retrospective, already about a self that has moved on. The loop closes inside a mind that is no longer in a position to act on the original choice.

Delay changes the shape of accountability. If the consequence comes late, it can be blamed on intervening factors. The original decision is no longer the only suspect. Incompleteness spreads responsibility across time, which makes it lighter and harder to grasp.

Partial confirmation changes the shape of conviction. A system that receives a small validation can treat it as a mandate. The confirmation becomes a story: "We were right." The absence of a full loop is hidden by the confidence of a partial loop.

The seduction is that partial confirmation feels like relief. It interrupts anxiety. It answers the immediate question even if it leaves the larger question unresolved. For a system under pressure, that interruption can feel like survival.

Perpetual anticipation changes the shape of attention. People tune their attention toward the next signal, the next review, the next release. The present becomes a staging area. If the loop is always about to close, then the moment of closure can be endlessly postponed without seeming dishonest.

The promise of closure becomes a moral resource. It justifies patience. It justifies sacrifice. It justifies silence. It makes the absence of proof look like prudence.

None of this requires overt manipulation. It can happen through routine procedures, through the natural friction of complex systems, through the ordinary desire to avoid panic. Incompleteness can be the accidental result of scale. But once it is present, it can also be protected.

Systems learn what kind of feedback threatens them. They develop reflexes around it. The reflexes can be procedural or cultural, explicit or implicit. What matters is that the loop that would create a decisive signal is made slower, noisier, or more distant.

The people inside the system often participate in this without noticing. They do not need to be cynical. They can be sincere, even idealistic. They can believe in the eventual closure of the loop, while also benefiting from the delay.

The belief in eventual closure is often genuine. The evidence is always "forthcoming." A report is being prepared. A data set is being cleaned. A test is being replicated. A policy is being evaluated. The loop remains open not because no one cares, but because caring is expressed as readiness rather than as proof.

This creates a particular type of trust. It is trust in the process, not trust in the outcome. Trust becomes fidelity to the machinery, not to the results. The system becomes trustworthy by appearing meticulous, even when it produces no final conclusion.

The machinery has an aesthetic. There are meetings, dashboards, metrics, ceremonies. Each of these can be true and still incomplete. A system can be transparent about its process and opaque about its reality. It can show every step and still avoid closure.

Incompleteness makes a system resilient to disconfirmation. A closed loop demands a reckoning. An incomplete loop allows reinterpretation. If the result is negative, it can be deemed premature. If the result is positive, it can be celebrated without being tested.

This is not simply bias. It is a structural advantage. In a world of competing narratives, the system that can keep its feedback ambiguous can keep its narrative alive. It does not have to be correct. It only has to be unclosed.

The people who build or maintain such systems often see themselves as responsible. They are not trying to evade truth. They are trying to manage risk. Complete feedback can be destabilizing. It can trigger blame, funding loss, reputational damage, or abrupt reversal.

When a full loop threatens collapse, incompleteness can feel like care. The system must be protected long enough to deliver value. The loop can be closed later, after stabilization. But later is always another moment, always a different set of people.

Incompleteness also distributes comfort. A system that promises closure in the future allows each person to believe they are doing their part. The discomfort of uncertainty is spread across time and across roles. No single person holds the full burden of doubt.

The danger is not that the loop never closes. The danger is that people adapt to a world in which closure is no longer expected. They begin to interpret absence of feedback as normal, even as evidence of correctness. The loop becomes not just open, but irrelevant.

Consider a long project whose success is always said to be "just ahead." The delays are explained as the price of ambition. The partial successes are highlighted as signs of life. The anticipation is nurtured through milestones that are meaningful in process but inconclusive in effect.

The project continues. People invest more time, more reputation, more identity. With each investment, the desire for a decisive loop grows, but so does the cost of a negative outcome. The system quietly shifts from seeking closure to maintaining the conditions of anticipation.

The same pattern can exist in relationships. One person keeps waiting for clarity, for acknowledgement, for an unambiguous response. The feedback comes in fragments. There is enough to keep hope alive, not enough to settle the question. The loop remains open, and the waiting becomes a way of life.

In professional life, incomplete loops can feel like a permanent provisional status. The promotion is being considered. The project is under review. The strategy is being assessed. Signals arrive, but they are equivocal. The person inside the system experiences their own competence through those signals and cannot fully locate it.

There is a special cruelty in partial confirmation. It does not deny you outright. It gives you a fragment of the recognition you seek, but not enough to stop you from seeking it. The loop becomes a device that keeps effort flowing without delivering resolution.

Delay, partial confirmation, and anticipation are not separate stages. They can be woven together so that the system feels both stable and dynamic. There is movement, but not closure. There is evidence, but not proof. There is waiting, but it feels like progress.

A loop that never closes can still be full of motion. It can be busy, crowded, and emotionally intense. It can provide a sense of purpose.

The energy is real. The feedback is incomplete. This combination is what makes it so durable.

The person inside such a loop experiences a specific kind of pressure. They are asked to respond to partial signals as if those signals were final. They are asked to treat delay as a natural feature. They are asked to keep investing in anticipation of a closure that remains distant.

The sensation is not always frustration. It can be devotion. The system gives meaning by constantly gesturing toward the moment when meaning will be confirmed. The person who stays is not necessarily naive. They may be interpreting the only available evidence.

Incomplete feedback reshapes the language of accountability. The question shifts from "What happened?" to "Where are we in the process?" Instead of demanding a result, the system requests an update. Updates are safe. Results are risky.

The update becomes a ritual of reassurance. It is a way to signal activity without forcing confrontation. It can be sincere and still function as a shield. It allows people to feel aligned even when they are uncertain.

Over time, the system learns to prefer updates to outcomes. The structure of work changes. Progress is defined as movement through stages rather than arrival at a destination. The loop does not close, but the path is mapped and celebrated.

Mapping the path gives a false kind of certainty. The milestones appear concrete. The dates are written down. The architecture is drawn. Each element reinforces the belief that the loop is in fact closing, just slowly. The impression is precise, but the result remains unconfirmed.

There is an important difference between a loop that is open and a loop that is hidden. An open loop can be acknowledged. A hidden loop is concealed by procedural theater. The system keeps its participants in activity so they do not have to confront the absence of closure.

The theater is often called "due diligence" or "rigor." It can be real, and still be incomplete. The effort is genuine. The closure is not. The system can proudly document the work and still avoid the decisive feedback that would change it.

Incompleteness has a particular way of resisting blame. If a loop never closes, there is no clear point of failure. There is only a series of delays and interruptions. Failure disperses into the background. It becomes an atmosphere rather than an event.

This dispersal is part of why the system survives. A closed loop exposes a mistake. An incomplete loop allows mistakes to be reinterpreted as ongoing challenges. The language of "learning" becomes a way to postpone judgment. Learning can be real and still indefinite.

The system remains alive because the future is always invited to correct the present. Correction is deferred, not denied. This is enough to keep participants engaged. It is also enough to keep critics unsure about when to insist.

The price is paid in the accumulation of unresolved obligations. Every incomplete loop leaves a residue. The residue is carried by people who are close enough to feel it but not powerful enough to close it. They hold the tension between promise and proof.

This is where entrapment deepens. The person closest to the loop feels responsible for its closure, even without the authority to force it. They are asked for updates, for reassurance, for patience, for interpretation. They become the caretaker of a gap they did not create.

Responsibility expands inside an incomplete loop. When the system refuses to close, someone must keep it open. The caretaker becomes part of the loop's survival. Their presence is evidence that the loop is still in motion. Their energy substitutes for closure.

The caretaker is often praised. They are dependable, calm, and committed. Those are real qualities. The system relies on them. The reliance can look like appreciation while quietly increasing the weight they carry.

Incompleteness also changes the emotional experience of time. Time is not a line but a spiral. You return to the same questions with slight adjustments. Each pass feels like progress. Each pass also confirms that the loop is still open.

The spiral is satisfying because it produces novelty without resolution. You can always say something new about why the loop has not closed. You can always point to a fresh variable, a new constraint, a different stakeholder. The explanation evolves, the closure does not.

This is not necessarily deception. Complex systems genuinely have evolving contexts. But evolving context can be used to deflect closure. Each new variable becomes a reason to wait. Each reason to wait becomes a reason to continue.

A system that keeps feedback incomplete becomes adept at redefining what counts as closure. It lowers the threshold when it needs praise and raises it when it faces judgment. The standard shifts gently, almost invisibly. The loop moves not because the world changed, but because the system's definition of success did.

The people inside the loop feel the shift but cannot easily name it. They know the target moved, but they do not know who moved it. No single person is responsible for the drift. It happens through accumulated reinterpretations. The loop never closes because the circle keeps stretching.

Partial confirmation is especially powerful when it aligns with identity. A team wants to believe it is competent. A leader wants to believe the vision is sound. A community wants to believe the sacrifice is meaningful. Partial confirmation provides a mirror. It reflects enough to sustain the identity.

That mirror does not need to be accurate. It only needs to be plausible. The system does not demand certainty. It asks for credibility. Credibility is easier to maintain in an incomplete loop because the final verdict is always ahead.

The incomplete loop also redistributes dissent. Criticism is not eliminated. It is delayed, softened, and redirected. A critic is told to wait for the upcoming review, the next data set, the updated analysis. The critique is not refuted. It is postponed.

Postponement can be framed as fairness. It can be framed as professionalism. It can be framed as care for accuracy. These framings are often sincere. They are also convenient. The loop remains open, the critique is suspended, the system continues.

The waiting becomes a social practice. People learn to speak in tentative terms. They learn to soften their claims. They learn to attach their conclusions to future evidence. The system rewards this caution because it keeps the loop open.

Yet the system also punishes the person who insists on closure. The insistence is labeled premature, disruptive, or simplistic. It threatens the rhythm of anticipation. It exposes the system to a verdict it has not prepared to absorb. The person who demands closure becomes the problem.

Perpetual anticipation has a distinctive emotional color. It is not despair. It is not satisfaction. It is a suspended readiness. It feels like the moment before a decision, stretched across months or years. That readiness can be exhausting, but it can also be addictive.

The system does not need to force anticipation. Anticipation can be self-generated. Humans are built to search for patterns and outcomes. When signals are partial, the mind fills in the rest. The loop stays open because the participants do the work of keeping it meaningful.

This is why incomplete feedback can be so enduring. It does not rely on a single authority. It recruits the psychology of its participants. It offers enough structure to feel legitimate and enough ambiguity to avoid closure. It becomes a habitat rather than a mechanism.

In that habitat, learning is constant but inconclusive. People attend trainings, read reports, discuss lessons. Each act suggests that the loop is closing. Each act can be folded into the structure without forcing a decision. Learning becomes another form of motion.

The consequence is a strange mix of earnestness and stasis. The system can be full of smart, well-meaning people. It can be full of work. It can be full of data. And yet it does not change its core direction because the decisive feedback never arrives.

This is not the same as laziness. Lazy systems are often simple to diagnose. Incomplete loops are not lazy. They are active, evolving, sophisticated. Their incompleteness is hidden beneath activity. It is easy to mistake motion for closure.

There is also a moral burden in incomplete loops. If closure never arrives, responsibility becomes a matter of interpretation rather than evidence. Who is responsible for an outcome that never fully materializes? The system answers with proximity and commitment. The people who stayed are held responsible for what never closed.

This creates a subtle coercion. Staying is treated as consent. Continuing is treated as agreement. If you are still here, you must believe in the loop. The system does not need to ask explicitly. Your presence is used as confirmation.

Partial confirmation can be used to draw outsiders in. A small success is publicized. A pilot is celebrated. A preliminary study is cited. Each signal is real, and each is incomplete. The system gains support without having to submit to full accountability.

This dynamic is visible in many domains. In technology, prototypes demonstrate possibility without proving reliability. In policy, early indicators justify continued funding while long-term effects remain unclear. In science, preliminary results attract attention before replication closes the loop. Each case is different, but the structure of incompleteness is familiar.

In science, delay is often noble. Complex questions take time. But delay can also be protective. It allows narratives to settle before evidence can challenge them. The longer the delay, the more the narrative is braided into identity. When the loop eventually closes, the system has already invested in a story.

In politics, incomplete feedback is not only common; it is almost necessary. Policies unfold over decades. Consequences are distributed across populations. No single election can close the loop. The result is a system that can claim progress or deny harm depending on which partial signals are emphasized.

In personal life, incomplete feedback is intimate. You do not fully know the effect you have on another person. You read cues, interpret silences, build assumptions. The loop never closes because the other person is not a controlled system. You live in partial confirmation and perpetual anticipation.

The entrapment here is not external. It is embedded in relationship itself. To care about another person is to accept incomplete feedback. The danger arises when that incompleteness is used to keep someone waiting without closure, when signals are given just enough to prevent departure.

The loop can also be incomplete by design. A system can be built to maximize engagement rather than resolution. If resolution ends engagement, then the system has an incentive to avoid it. It can deliver small rewards, delayed outcomes, and endless anticipation. The feedback remains incomplete because completion would end the cycle that sustains it.

This is visible in entertainment, in communication platforms, in educational systems. Each has reasons to keep participants involved. Each can be structured to provide progress without closure. It is not always cynical. It is often a byproduct of how value is measured.

Value is often measured in activity. Activity is easy to count. Closure is harder to define. When metrics privilege motion, the system learns to produce motion. Feedback becomes another form of activity rather than a decisive signal. The loop turns without ending.

In such systems, ambiguity is not a flaw. It is a resource. Ambiguity allows multiple narratives to coexist. It allows the system to satisfy different stakeholders without resolving their contradictions. Closure would force a choice. Incompleteness preserves flexibility.

Flexibility has benefits. It can protect against premature conclusions. It can keep a system adaptive. But it can also prevent any conclusion from being treated as binding. The loop never closes because closing would mean losing flexibility.

This is why incomplete loops can appear rational. They allow adjustment. They prevent brittle decisions. They maintain optionality. These are legitimate advantages. The cost is that optionality can become a permanent mode, and decisions can become non-decisions.

Non-decisions are still decisions. They allocate time, attention, and resources. They privilege certain outcomes while pretending to remain neutral. The loop remains open, but the system is moving in a direction. Incompleteness hides the directionality by avoiding explicit closure.

The person inside the loop often senses this. They feel the drift. They see the direction. But they are told the system is still evaluating. Their sense is not enough to close the loop. They are asked to keep waiting.

Waiting in a system is not passive. It is labor. It requires emotional regulation, attention management, repeated recalibration of expectations. The person who waits is doing work. That work is often invisible, which makes it easy to demand more of it.

Because the work is invisible, it is also easy to interpret it as consent. If you are still waiting, you must accept the terms. If you are still engaged, you must believe the loop will close. This interpretation is not fair, but it is common. The system uses it to secure compliance without explicit agreement.

Incompleteness can also be a function of competing loops. A person may be inside several loops at once, each with its own delays and partial signals. Feedback from one loop is used to justify patience in another. The loops reinforce each other by keeping the person busy, and the busy-ness makes it difficult to notice the absence of closure.

The wider environment can normalize incomplete feedback. If everyone around you is waiting, then waiting feels normal. If everyone is posting updates, then updates feel like progress. Social comparison stabilizes the loop. It makes the absence of closure less alarming.

This normalization can be institutional. An organization can build roles that exist primarily to manage incompleteness. There are coordinators, liaisons, program managers, facilitators. These roles can be crucial. They can also become the human infrastructure of an open loop. The system stays open because it has people whose job is to keep it moving.

The presence of infrastructure makes the loop feel real. It creates a sense of seriousness. It signals investment. It can make the demand for closure feel unreasonable because the system is already so elaborate. The more infrastructure, the harder it is to admit that the loop is still open.

An incomplete loop also distorts memory. When closure never arrives, people create narratives to explain why. Those narratives become the record. Later, when someone asks what happened, the story is already settled, even though the loop never closed.

This narrative stabilization is not the same as truth. It is a coping mechanism. It makes the uncertainty bearable. It allows people to move forward. But it also makes the system less responsive to new information, because the story has already been told.

The system becomes a story about itself. It tells a story of progress, of learning, of eventual closure. People align with the story because alignment is rewarded. The story can be sincere and still function as a shield. It protects the system from the demands of final feedback.

When a loop does close, it can be traumatic. The closure arrives like a verdict. It collapses the ambiguity that allowed so many interpretations. The system that has lived in anticipation is forced into a single, definitive account. This is often resisted, not because the truth is unwanted, but because the suddenness is destabilizing.

To avoid that destabilization, the system learns to treat closure as dangerous. It may frame closure as "oversimplification." It may frame closure as "politicized." It may frame closure as "premature." The labels are sometimes accurate. They are also protective. The loop stays open.

The person inside the loop can feel this protection as suffocation. They want clarity, but they also fear the consequences of clarity. They are asked to be patient, to be reasonable, to be loyal to the process. They are also asked to bear the tension of incompleteness. This tension is not evenly distributed.

Those with the least authority often bear the most tension. They are closest to the action and furthest from the decision. They see the gap between promise and outcome but cannot close it. They are asked to translate ambiguity into reassurance for others. The loop remains open, and they become its translators.

Translation is a form of responsibility. It requires judgment. It is not merely passing along information. It is interpreting incomplete signals and presenting them as coherent. The translator carries the emotional weight of that interpretation. They are accountable for clarity even when clarity does not exist.

This is how incomplete loops deepen entrapment. The people who are most capable of holding ambiguity are asked to hold more of it. Their competence is converted into obligation. They become necessary to the system's survival, which makes it harder for them to step away.

Incompleteness can also be mistaken for complexity. Complexity is real. Some questions do require long horizons and nuanced evidence. But incompleteness is not the same as complexity. A system can use complexity as a shield, insisting that closure is impossible even when it is merely inconvenient.

There is an ethical ambiguity here. Demanding closure in a complex system can be reckless. Refusing closure can be evasive. The distinction is difficult to make from inside. It requires judgment. Judgment does not operate like a method. It is not reproducible. It depends on attention, experience, and a sense of proportion.

This is why the chapter is not a guide to escaping loops. It is an attempt to name what it feels like to live inside one. The point is not to provide a route out. The point is to clarify why the route is not obvious. Incomplete feedback is not an error you can simply correct. It is a condition you must interpret.

Interpretation is contested. Different people will read the same partial signals in different ways. One sees evidence of progress. Another sees evidence of avoidance. Both can be plausible. The system can continue because disagreement prevents closure. Ambiguity does not just slow the loop. It creates multiple loops, each with its own direction.

The system can even use disagreement as a resource. If there is no consensus on what the feedback means, then the feedback cannot force a decision. The loop remains open because interpretation remains open. The system survives by keeping meaning unsettled.

The language of "pilot" and "trial" is emblematic. It offers a future closure. It protects the present from the verdict of failure. If the pilot goes well, it becomes proof. If the pilot goes poorly, it becomes a preliminary experiment. The loop never closes because the frame is designed to keep it tentative.

Tentativeness can be virtuous. It can prevent overconfidence. But when tentativeness becomes permanent, it is a way of avoiding accountability. The system can claim humility while continuing unchanged. The loop stays open not because humility is needed, but because closure would be costly.

Cost is often the hidden driver. Closing a loop can be expensive. It can require admitting mistakes, reallocating resources, or disrupting entrenched roles. An incomplete loop spreads those costs across time. It allows the system to postpone payment. The debt accumulates, but it remains abstract.

The abstractness is key. Concrete feedback compels action. Abstract feedback invites interpretation. If the data is messy, if the outcomes are diffuse, the loop can remain open. The system can continue to operate under the banner of "more study needed." This is sometimes true. It is also sometimes convenient.

A system that never closes its loops can still achieve local successes. It can solve small problems, improve processes, learn microlessons. Those successes can be genuine. They can also be used to justify the absence of a larger verdict. The system points to the small wins as evidence that the big question is being addressed. The loop remains open.

This is a kind of survival strategy. By remaining incomplete, the system remains adaptable. It can pivot without admitting error. It can incorporate new information without acknowledging that the old information was misleading. It can rewrite its own history. An open loop is more flexible than a closed one.

Flexibility has a cost for the people who rely on the system for clarity. Their lives may be organized around the promise of closure. They may need a decision to move on, to commit, to stop waiting. In an incomplete loop, those needs are deferred. The deferral is not only logistical. It is psychological.

The psychology is shaped by hope and fear. Hope keeps people engaged. Fear keeps them cautious. The system feeds both by providing partial confirmation and delayed consequences. People oscillate between optimism and anxiety, and the oscillation itself becomes normal. The loop does not close because the emotional energy keeps it moving.

There is also a prestige associated with being inside a long, open loop. It suggests involvement in something complex and significant. Being part of a project that never quite resolves can feel like being part of history in the making. This prestige can mask the costs of incompleteness. It can turn waiting into a badge.

The badge is reinforced by language. People speak of "journeys," "transformations," "roadmaps," "evolutions." These terms signal motion without specifying a destination. They are not wrong. They are also perfect for a system that benefits from remaining open. The loop becomes a narrative arc rather than a circuit.

Narrative arcs do not need closure in the same way that loops do. They can end in ambiguity. They can be episodic. They can be renewed in sequels. A system that adopts narrative logic can continue indefinitely. It can keep participants engaged by providing chapters instead of conclusions.

This chapter itself is part of a narrative. It is not a verdict. It is an attempt to describe a structure that resists verdicts. The reader may feel recognition. Recognition is a kind of feedback, but it is not closure. It does not tell you what to do. It tells you what you are seeing.

The need for recognition is significant. People inside incomplete loops often feel isolated. They are surrounded by activity but lack a shared language for the experience. Naming the pattern can reduce that isolation. But naming is not the same as closing. It is a way of holding the ambiguity with more clarity.

Clarity is not the same as control. You can understand the loop and still be inside it. You can see the delays, the partial confirmations, the perpetual anticipation, and still be bound by them. Understanding does not automatically free you. That is part of the trap.

The trap is not always imposed. It can be chosen, consciously or not. A person may prefer the open loop to the risk of a definitive outcome. A system may prefer to keep options alive rather than commit to a path. Incompleteness is sometimes safer than clarity. Safety can be seductive.

The seductive quality is intensified when the loop is connected to identity. If your role, your community, or your purpose is bound up with a process, closing the loop can feel like erasing yourself. A system that never closes allows identity to remain intact. It offers continuity. It postpones the reckoning that would require change.

This does not mean the system is dishonest. It means the system is alive to the costs of finality. Finality is not just a conclusion. It is a redistribution of power, a reallocation of meaning, a reshaping of narrative. An open loop avoids that upheaval. It chooses endurance over decisiveness.

Endurance can be valuable. Some problems require it. Some questions cannot be settled quickly. The danger is when endurance becomes an excuse for endlessness. The line between patience and avoidance is thin. From inside the system, that line is often invisible.

From the outside, it can look obvious. But outsiders are not the ones carrying the consequences of closure. They do not bear the costs of disruption, the loss of legitimacy, the fracture of relationships. The system is maintained by those who are invested. Their investment is precisely what makes closure risky.

This is why judgment in such systems is difficult. It is not enough to know that the loop is incomplete. One must also understand why it remains open, what it protects, and what it postpones. Those questions do not have formulaic answers. They require sensitivity to context, to history, to human cost.

A person may be told that closure is coming, that the next cycle will finally resolve the question. They may have heard this before. They may still believe it. Belief is not irrational. It can be the only way to make the present bearable. The loop is held together by that belief.

Belief is strengthened by partial confirmation. A small win arrives. A problem seems to shrink. A respected figure expresses confidence. Each signal fuels the anticipation. The system does not need certainty. It needs enough evidence to keep belief alive.

The loop can also be sustained by fear of disappointment. If closure arrives and the outcome is negative, the investment may feel wasted. People may prefer the ambiguity of an open loop to the pain of a definitive failure. This preference is understandable. It is also a mechanism of entrapment.

Entrapment deepens not through coercion but through accumulation. Each delay, each partial confirmation, each anticipated review adds another layer of commitment. The layers are not easily peeled away. The loop becomes part of how life is organized. Closing it would require reconfiguring not just a decision, but a way of being.

This is why incomplete loops can last for years. The longer they last, the more they shape their participants. They teach people to live in provisional time. They teach people to build identity around process. They teach people to interpret uncertainty as normal. By the time closure becomes possible, the system has already adapted to its absence.

There is a paradox here. Incomplete feedback can make a system appear stable, because nothing forces change. But it also makes the system fragile, because reality is not being integrated. When closure finally arrives, it can be catastrophic. The system has been living on anticipation. The verdict interrupts the narrative.

The interruption is often experienced as betrayal. People are not only disappointed in the outcome. They are disappointed in the process that promised them an eventual answer. The system feels like it broke a contract, even if the contract was never explicit. The loop closes, and the meaning collapses.

This collapse can produce a cynical response. People may conclude that all feedback is political, that closure is always deferred, that the system was never real. This cynicism is itself a kind of feedback. It can close the loop in a destructive way by withdrawing participation. Yet the system may survive even this by appealing to a new generation with a renewed promise of eventual closure.

The renewal is often sincere. People who join later may not know the history. They engage with the process, find the partial confirmations, wait for the anticipated closure. The loop begins again. This is one way that incomplete systems perpetuate themselves over time. They cycle through people, not through conclusions.

The moral complexity of this is real. Some systems deserve to survive because they are working on hard problems. Others survive because incompleteness shields them from accountability. The same structure can serve both. Incompleteness is not a verdict in itself. It is a condition that can be used for care or for evasion.

Understanding that condition requires attention to signals that are not decisive. It requires the ability to sit with ambiguity without collapsing into premature certainty. It requires a sensitivity to how delay, partial confirmation, and anticipation shape behavior. This sensitivity is a form of judgment. It is not a method that can be transferred wholesale. It depends on context and experience.

In many systems, the feedback that matters most is also the hardest to measure. The system relies on proxies, and proxies create a structural incompleteness. A dashboard may show motion while the underlying reality remains murky. The numbers are not false, but they are partial. They provide a confirmation that can be comforting precisely because it is limited.

Proxies tend to harden into habits. Once a proxy is in place, it becomes a target for attention. People optimize for the signal they can see. The unseen consequences arrive later, or not at all. The loop stays open because the system is looking at its own reflection.

Legal and investigative processes demonstrate another texture of delay. Due process exists to protect fairness, and fairness takes time. That time can be honorable. It can also become a shield against reckoning. When decisions are always pending, responsibility can be paused. The loop remains open under the banner of procedural care.

In education, feedback arrives in cycles that are long by design. A semester, a year, a degree, a career. Assessment is episodic. The evidence of learning is partial, filtered through grades and credentials. A person can move through the system with a sense of progress while the deeper loop of understanding never fully closes.

In health, the incompleteness is often visceral. Chronic conditions improve and worsen. Treatments show promise, then recede. A symptom fades without explanation, a new one appears. The feedback is intimate, yet ambiguous. The loop never closes because the body is not a simple instrument with a single verdict.

Public attention creates its own incomplete loops. A headline functions as an initial feedback signal. Corrections or long-term outcomes arrive later, if they arrive at all. The early signal shapes perception, and the later signal struggles to overwrite it. The loop remains open because attention has moved on.

Incomplete loops also shape language over time. People begin to speak in conditional terms, to hedge their claims, to anchor their statements to pending results. This language can be cautious and responsible. It can also become a way to avoid saying anything that could be tested. The loop stays open because the vocabulary of closure is no longer practiced.

The emotional economy of incomplete feedback is uneven. Those who are rewarded for patience develop a tolerance for ambiguity. Those who are not rewarded feel the cost more sharply. This difference can fracture communities. Some become invested in the open loop as a source of stability, while others experience it as abandonment.

Rituals emerge to manage the tension. There are annual reviews, periodic retrospectives, commemorations of milestones. These rituals can be meaningful. They can also function as substitutes for closure. A ritual can give the feeling of resolution without changing the underlying loop.

The longer a loop remains open, the more memory itself becomes part of the system. People recall the early promises, the partial confirmations, the missed closures. Memory adds weight to the present. It can deepen commitment or deepen doubt. Either way, it ties the participant more tightly to the loop.

The reader may want a way to close the loop. The desire is understandable. But the chapter does not offer that. It offers a description of the mechanisms by which loops remain open, and of the ways those mechanisms bind people inside them. The description is meant to clarify, not to instruct. It is meant to show why the loop feels so hard to close from within.

Perhaps the clearest sign of an incomplete loop is the persistence of a question that should have been settled long ago. Yet even that is not a rule. Some questions persist because they are profound. Others persist because the system cannot afford to settle them. Discerning which is which is a matter of judgment, not technique.

The chapter ends where the loop continues. There is no tidy closure here. That is appropriate. A chapter about incomplete feedback should not pretend to resolve what it describes. If it did, it would participate in the very dynamic it critiques. It would offer a satisfying ending rather than an honest account.

So the loop remains open. The reader carries the recognition, perhaps with a sharper sense of the delays, the partial confirmations, and the anticipations that structure their own systems. Recognition is not liberation, but it is a form of clarity. Clarity can be a quiet companion inside an open loop. It does not close the circuit. It allows you to see the wires.

Chapter 6

Why systems quietly reward over-responsibility

Most systems do not explicitly ask individuals to carry excessive responsibility.

That absence is part of the mechanism. The transfer of responsibility is framed as voluntary, even when the expectation is steady and the consequences of refusal are real. The language that signals the transfer is moral rather than procedural. Words such as "responsible" or "step up" describe character more than assignment. They invite the person to treat responsibility as a reflection of who they are, not of what they are authorized to do. The system can then rely on self assignment without issuing a directive. The more the person identifies with that moral frame, the less the system needs to manage allocation directly.

Calling it a control surface is not to suggest a machine with levers but to note the practicality of language as interface. A shift in tone can move responsibility without reassigning roles. A manager who says "I know you'll handle it" or a peer who says "you always come through" changes the distribution of effort with a sentence. These phrases do not grant authority, yet they shape behavior. The surface is calibrated by praise, disappointment, and the implied standard of what a good member does. It is low cost, responsive, and hard to contest. That is why it is so effective at stabilizing where responsibility lands.

The frame is also protective. A system that never explicitly assigns excessive responsibility can plausibly deny it. It can present itself as fair and balanced while still benefiting from a pattern in which one or two people repeatedly take on the uncertain and the urgent. The moral language does not merely describe; it produces the internal push that fills gaps. Responsibility is positioned as a virtue, and virtue seeks proof. The person who wants to be good steps forward, often before they have asked what authority accompanies the act.

Responsibility as virtue carries a particular weight. It collapses the difference between capability and obligation. A capable person becomes a person who ought to act. The system does not need to say "take this" when the person has already accepted that not taking it would be a moral blemish. The language of virtue turns optional work into an identity test. The person does not merely help; they confirm who they are. That confirmation can feel like agency even as it tightens the system's reliance.

They simply make it advantageous to do so.

Advantage is rarely a formal reward. It is relief in the room, a quiet nod, the sense that you kept things from getting worse. These micro rewards are not documented, but they accumulate as social capital. The moral vocabulary becomes a control surface, a set of cues that shifts responsibility to the person most willing to absorb it. The surface is smooth to the system and sticky to the individual: the system glides forward, while the individual collects the adhesive of obligation. The advantage is also psychological. The person who carries responsibility can feel necessary, and necessity can feel like belonging.

That sense of belonging is reinforced through public gratitude. The system often produces ceremonies of appreciation, small or large, that signal a person's importance. These gestures feel affirming, but they do not alter decision rights or resource allocation. Praise is inexpensive; power is not. When praise substitutes for power, it allows the system to access more labor while avoiding the structural consequences of making that labor formal. The person receives recognition but not the authority to reshape the conditions that required the extra responsibility.

Over-responsibility is rarely mandated.

A mandate would require the system to account for decision rights, capacity, and support. It would require an explicit acknowledgment that the system is placing more on one person than on another. That explicitness is what most systems avoid, because it would expose the imbalance. Instead, the moral frame allows the

155

system to access extra effort while keeping its own self description intact. The person is not ordered to do more; they are praised for doing more. The absence of a mandate is not a neutral space. It is a space filled with expectation, and expectation has a tone.

Mandates are costly because they create explicit accountability. If the system assigned the burden formally, it would also be responsible for the support that burden requires. By keeping the burden informal, the system keeps its own obligations ambiguous. The moral frame carries that ambiguity. It makes the extra responsibility look like initiative rather than assignment, which means the system can benefit without admitting that it demanded anything. This ambiguity is another stabilizer; it keeps responsibility in motion without ever placing it on paper.

It is incentivized.

The incentives are social and reputational, and they are wrapped in virtue. People who carry more are described as trustworthy, mature, stable, reliable. These adjectives are not neutral. They are moral judgments about a person's character, and they attach status to the act of over responsibility. The person may not gain power, but they gain a kind of honor. The system can then continue to draw on that honor to ask for more, without ever issuing a directive. Incentive and virtue become fused, and the person experiences both as the same pressure.

Incentive here is a matter of standing. The person who absorbs more is invited into more conversations, consulted more often, treated as someone who can be counted on. That standing is valuable because it promises influence, even if it never delivers it. The moral frame wraps the standing in virtue and makes it feel earned. The person sees the standing as evidence of their character, and the system can point to that character when it needs someone to step in again.

Standing is maintained through repeated moral tests. A person is given a chance to prove responsibility, and their response becomes part of their story. The story is less about the task than about the signal it sends. When the person accepts the task, they are seen as reliable. When they hesitate, the system may reinterpret that hesitation as a shift in character. This moral reading of behavior is how the incentive persists. It makes responsibility feel like something one must continually re-earn.

The incentives are subtle, often invisible, and almost never documented.

Subtlety is how a system keeps its control surface clean. The incentives are delivered through tone, timing, and silence as much as through explicit praise. A delayed response to someone who declines, a quick thanks to someone who absorbs, a story told later about who saved the day. These cues are invisible in policy and unmistakable in practice. They are easy to feel and hard to quote. Because they are not documented, they are difficult to challenge without seeming petty or defensive. The invisible nature of the incentives is precisely what makes them durable. They operate beneath formal accountability, where they can be denied as misunderstanding or personality.

Shame without accusation works through absence rather than confrontation. When someone does not step in, the reaction is often a silence, a sigh, a half joke about "ownership," or a subtle shift in how their reliability is discussed. There is no formal blame to contest. The person senses that they have fallen short of a moral expectation without being told exactly what that expectation was. The vagueness is protective for the system and powerful for the individual, who fills the gap with self doubt.

Documentation would require the system to admit that it values certain moral behaviors over others. It would have to say, explicitly, that it prefers those who take on extra load and smooth disruption. That kind of clarity would also require compensation or authority. By keeping the incentives unspoken, the system keeps itself from having to match words with structural change. The moral framing does the work quietly, transferring effort while leaving no trace in official records.

The unspoken incentive structure is also easier to adjust. Praise can be intensified in a crisis and withdrawn afterward without explanation. Recognition can be given to a person without granting any authority to change underlying conditions. This flexibility is why moral language is a favored control surface. It allows the system to steer effort without the administrative cost of redesigning roles. The person may feel seen, yet the system remains unchanged.

Because the cues are moral, the person begins to supervise themselves. They anticipate the praise they might lose, the disappointment they might trigger, and adjust their behavior accordingly. This self monitoring is efficient for the system because it replaces overt control with internal discipline. The person is not told to take on more; they are guided to feel that taking on more is consistent with their character. The system can then rely on a steady supply of extra effort without escalating demands. The moral frame creates a kind of quiet contract between the person's identity and the system's needs.

Consider what happens when someone steps in to prevent failure.

The moment is often chaotic: a deadline that was never realistic, a decision that was never made, a gap between teams that no one owns. The person who steps in is responding to a sense of imminent loss, and the response is framed as care. They act not only because they want the outcome to improve, but because the moral narrative says a responsible person does not let things fall apart. The act is immediate and concrete. It produces a visible result that the system can see.

In those moments, other people often pause. They are not necessarily unwilling; they are uncertain about whether they are allowed to act. The person who steps in resolves that uncertainty for everyone else. The act is experienced as relief, and relief itself carries moral weight. The group feels gratitude, which then attaches to the person as a sign of virtue. The system learns who will absorb risk, and the moral frame marks that person as someone who should do it again.

The immediate outcome improves. The incident is resolved. The system moves on.

The resolution is experienced as a restoration of normality. The system does not linger on the conditions that made the intervention necessary. It takes the improved outcome as evidence that the system, broadly, still works. The person who intervened is often described as "handling it" rather than as creating an unplanned patch. The language turns a structural gap into a moment of personal competence. That conversion is not accidental. It allows the system to celebrate the outcome without examining the cause.

Afterward, the retelling usually highlights the person rather than the gap. The phrase "thanks for owning that" appears in conversations because it both recognizes the effort and closes the inquiry. The moral framing wraps the event in a story of responsibility, which makes it easy to move on. The structural question of who should have been responsible is displaced by the personal question of who was responsible. The person becomes the answer, and the system preserves its image.

From the system's perspective, this is success.

Success also carries a script for recognition. The person is thanked, sometimes publicly, and the thanks often closes the discussion. The recognition does not carry decision rights or a clearer role; it carries a sense that the system is grateful. Gratitude is meaningful, but it does not change the next crisis. The next time a gap appears, the system will again look toward the person who was thanked, because the thanks signaled who was responsible. Praise without power becomes a way to mark the responsible person without having to reorganize around them.

Success here is defined by continuity. The system values that the trajectory was preserved, not that the decision rights were clarified. Moral language helps that definition stick. The person is praised for being accountable, and the system sees itself as having accountable people. The act is interpreted as evidence of culture, not as evidence of risk. The moral frame stabilizes the placement of responsibility by defining the response as a personal virtue rather than a structural anomaly.

Continuity makes responsibility placement look stable. Once a person is identified as the stabilizer, the system can coordinate around that expectation. The moral label becomes a coordinate in the system's map. It is easier to route pressure toward the person who has already proven willing to carry it than to renegotiate roles in a tense moment. The system does not need to decide who should be responsible; it simply notices who has been. Moral framing makes past behavior appear like a trait, which makes future allocation feel obvious.

No audit follows.

An audit would ask questions the moral narrative does not want asked. It would inquire about why the risk appeared, who was supposed to decide, and whether the person who stepped in should have had to. It would ask about capacity and compensation. The absence of audit is not a failure of curiosity. It is a protection of the story. The story is clean: a responsible person did the right thing. Auditing would contaminate that clarity with complexity.

No question is asked about whether that person had the authority to act. No adjustment is made to prevent recurrence.

Authority is slow, and asking about it introduces the possibility that the act was inappropriate. The moral frame avoids that. It assumes that good intent overrides formal boundaries. That assumption is flattering to the person and convenient to the system. Preventing recurrence would require the system to formalize responsibility. Instead, the system accepts the patch as evidence that the moral fabric is strong enough to handle future disruptions.

When authority is questioned, it can feel like distrust. The person who asks whether they are allowed to act can be seen as less committed to the outcome. The moral framing makes authorization seem like an unnecessary barrier erected by someone who cares more about boundaries than about people. This interpretation does not require anyone to say it aloud; it is enough for the atmosphere to shift. That shift discourages the insistence on authority and keeps responsibility flowing toward those who will cross the boundary quietly.

The intervention becomes an invisible patch.

The patch also creates a form of moral debt. Others feel indebted to the person who saved the moment, which can lead to deference and continued reliance. The indebtedness is emotional rather than structural. It does not redistribute work; it deepens the expectation that the same person will save the next moment too. The system benefits from this informal obligation because it is durable and unrecorded. The person becomes the guardian of stability, and the system continues to build on that guardianship.

It disappears into the record as a success rather than a deviation. The patch is invisible because it is moralized. What looks like a personal act of responsibility is, in effect, a structural workaround. The moral language turns a workaround into a virtue. That makes it easy to repeat and difficult to challenge, because challenging it can be construed as challenging responsibility itself.

Over time, the system accumulates such patches. Each one is small and individually admirable, and together they become the informal architecture of how things get done. The system relies on that informal architecture precisely because it is invisible. It does not have to explain it, fund it, or even recognize it. The person who provides the patch sees the accumulated burden, but the system sees only continued stability.

Systems remember outcomes, not costs.

Memory in a system is rarely emotional; it is logistical. It lives in reports, metrics, and stories told upward. Those channels preserve the outcome and let the cost fade. When the outcome is acceptable, the internal strain required to produce it is treated as a private matter. The system is not malicious in this forgetting. It is simply built to retain what is visible and forget what is not. The hidden costs are carried in people, not in records.

What is remembered is also what is praised. Reports tend to highlight the responsible person rather than the conditions that made the responsibility necessary. The story of who carried responsibility becomes part of institutional memory, and that memory becomes a precedent. The next time a similar gap appears, the remembered name is the one that comes to mind. The moral framing thus shapes memory, and memory shapes placement.

The costs are not only fatigue. They are also the loss of opportunities to build better structures. When one person repeatedly absorbs responsibility, the system loses the chance to learn how to distribute it. Skills remain concentrated, knowledge remains centralized, and others remain unpracticed. The moral frame makes this concentration look like dedication rather than like a bottleneck. The cost is borne in the future as much as in the present, but the system's memory is too short to store that kind of cost.

Relational costs also accumulate. The person who repeatedly absorbs responsibility can become the bottleneck through which information flows. Others may defer, waiting for the responsible person to decide or act. That deference reduces shared ownership and can dampen initiative in the rest of the group. Creativity is narrowed because the same person is always solving the immediate crisis. The moral frame interprets the bottleneck as dedication rather than as a system constraint, which is why the cost can persist without correction.

If the outcome is acceptable, the internal strain required to produce it is irrelevant.

That irrelevance is not absolute, but it is operational. The system does not have a place to store the cost in its formal memory, so it does not become part of the decision context. The moral frame makes this easier. If someone chose to be responsible, then the strain can be interpreted as personal sacrifice, and personal sacrifice is not a system variable. It is part of the virtue story. The more responsibility is presented as a moral quality, the more cost is absorbed as a personal test rather than a collective problem.

When responsibility is tied to virtue, strain is interpreted as personal weakness rather than as evidence of overload. The person who struggles can feel ashamed, and that shame is internal because no one has accused them. The shame without accusation reinforces the pattern: the person seeks to repair their moral standing by taking on more, which deepens the burden. The system does not have to push; the moral frame pulls from within.

This creates a reinforcement loop.

The person who absorbs responsibility is seen as dependable. That visibility increases the likelihood that they will be relied upon again. The system begins to shape itself around their presence, subtly adjusting expectations and timelines in ways that assume the same person will step in when needed. The moral narrative intensifies. The person becomes known as reliable, and reliability becomes part of their identity. Identity then feeds back into behavior. The loop is not enforced by a formal mechanism; it is reinforced by recognition and expectation.

Dependability becomes a social contract. The system treats it as a promise, even if no promise was made. The person may be invited into discussions as a trusted figure, but trust does not equal authority. The system can lean on their judgment while still reserving the right to overrule or ignore it. This is praise without power. The person is respected for their reliability, yet their ability to change the conditions that create the need for reliability remains limited.

The contract is asymmetric. The dependable person is held to a higher bar, while others are excused by the mere absence of criticism. When the dependable person falters, the disappointment is sharper because it is a moral disappointment. The system relies on the person not only for output but for the sense that someone is taking care. That reliance deepens the pressure, and the moral frame makes the pressure feel like a test of character rather than a signal of overload.

Those who absorb responsibility stabilize the system. The system, in turn, stabilizes their position—temporarily.

Stability is offered as a reward, but it is a fragile reward. The person becomes a fixed point in the system's mental map. Their role is stabilized not by authority but by reliance. They are kept close because the system needs their capacity, not because it has decided to share power. The stabilization is temporary because it depends on continued absorption. If the person falters, the system will seek another absorber. The moral frame masks this contingency by treating responsibility as a permanent trait rather than a temporary choice.

They become "key people." "Go-to contacts." "Critical nodes."

These labels sound positive.

They are also functional. They map the system's dependency onto a person without naming it as dependency. The labels imply strength, but they also imply that the person is load bearing. The person is praised for being central, while the system avoids admitting that it has allowed the center to narrow. The moral language does the work of gratitude while keeping the structural imbalance intact.

The labels carry social gravity. People route questions, decisions, and worries toward the labeled person because the label implies capability. The person becomes a magnet for responsibility not because of a formal rule but because of the moral expectation embedded in the label. This magnetism can feel flattering at first, yet it pulls more and more load toward the same point. The system becomes quieter when the magnet is present, which is precisely what it values.

Labels are sticky. Once someone is known as the "go to" person, the label can outlast changes in workload, role, or capacity. People continue to route issues to them because the label is easier than reconsidering the distribution of responsibility. The label becomes a shortcut for coordination, and shortcuts are hard to abandon. The moral frame makes the shortcut feel like respect, which discourages reconsideration even when the burden has become unreasonable.

They are rarely neutral.

A neutral label would describe a role. These labels describe a person's moral standing in the system. They are respected, sometimes admired, and occasionally envied. But respect does not alter the burden. Admiration does not redistribute risk. The labels can even become a trap, because losing them feels like losing value. Praise without power is still praise, and it can be hard to refuse, but it is not authority.

Being indispensable is often mistaken for being valued.

Indispensability feels like validation because it creates attention. People notice when you are absent, and that notice can feel like care. Yet care is not the same as protection. To be indispensable is to be necessary for the system to remain stable, which means the system has allowed itself to become dependent. Dependency is not an award. It is a vulnerability. The moral frame often hides this, because it speaks in the language of trust and loyalty.

In reality, indispensability is a structural vulnerability. It concentrates risk while diffusing accountability.

The concentrated risk sits in the person, while accountability diffuses back into the system. If something fails, the indispensable person is visible. If things succeed, the system can claim the success as collective. The moral narrative makes this feel fair because the responsible person is celebrated, but celebration does not change the distribution of exposure. The person's value is real, yet it is expressed in a way that isolates them rather than strengthens their position.

Diffused accountability also means that failure is personalized while success is socialized. The system can point to the individual when something goes wrong, because the individual was the one who stepped in. When things go well, the system can point to its culture. The moral frame makes this feel natural. It praises responsibility when it produces stability and assigns responsibility when stability fails. In both cases, the individual remains the focal point.

Systems also reward speed.

Speed is a virtue in environments where uncertainty is high and coordination is costly. It looks like competence and confidence. It is easy to praise and hard to oppose. The moral vocabulary quickly attaches to speed: "decisive," "proactive," "can be counted on." These are assessments of character. They imply that slowness is not only inefficient but also irresponsible. The system learns to favor the person who moves quickly, especially when that speed prevents a visible failure.

Over-responsibility is fast.

It bypasses deliberation by substituting one person's judgment for shared decision making. It compresses the time of uncertainty. It gives the system an answer before the system has asked the question. In doing so, it becomes a moral service. The person is not just efficient; they are virtuous for protecting others from the discomfort of waiting. The reward for speed is not only the outcome; it is the reinforcing story that good people act quickly.

It bypasses deliberation. It avoids escalation. It eliminates friction.

These qualities are attractive to the system because they reduce coordination costs. They are also morally coded as helpfulness and maturity. To slow down and insist on authority can feel like withholding. The person who absorbs responsibility takes that moral risk away from the group. They become the adult in the room, and that role is rewarded by respect even when it comes without support.

Friction can be moralized as negativity. The person who slows the process may be described as "blocking" or "complicating" without a direct accusation. The language implies that they are not being helpful. This is shame without accusation: no one says the person is wrong, but the tone suggests that they are not aligned with the group's values. The person who absorbs responsibility avoids that risk and is rewarded for doing so.

Formal authority, by contrast, is slow.

Authority requires explicit permission, documentation, and the possibility of disagreement. It is messy because it exposes the actual structure of power. It forces the system to confront whether it has provided the necessary clarity and resources. From a moral perspective, authority can be framed as self protection, while speed can be framed as selflessness. The moral vocabulary thus tilts the field toward speed, even when authority would be more sustainable.

When the moral frame favors selflessness, authority can seem self interested. The person who asks for clarity can be cast as someone who cares more about their position than about the outcome. This framing is subtle, often unstated, yet it is powerful. It pushes responsibility toward those who are willing to act without clarity, even when that action would be better supported with it. The system benefits from the immediate action, and the moral frame keeps the imbalance hidden.

It requires clarification. It triggers review. It introduces the possibility of refusal.

Each of these is a point where the system could be forced to look at itself. Clarification asks who decides. Review asks who is accountable. Refusal asks what happens when someone does not comply. These questions are structurally important but emotionally uncomfortable. The person who bypasses them is praised for keeping the system calm. The moral frame rewards the calm, not the clarity.

From a system optimization perspective, speed wins.

Optimization here is not mathematical; it is felt. The system experiences speed as reduced friction and reduced exposure. The short term gain is easily measured, while the long term cost is distributed and delayed. Moral language helps keep this weighting in place. The person who moves quickly is seen as virtuous, and virtue becomes a proxy for effectiveness. This proxy allows the system to ignore the slower, structural work that would redistribute responsibility more evenly.

In moments of pressure, the moral signals intensify. Words like "need" and "step up" become more frequent, praise becomes more immediate, and silence around limits becomes louder. The control surface is adjusted to route pressure toward those who will absorb it. The system may not be aware that it is doing this; it simply reacts with the language it has. The result is a stable placement of responsibility in the same hands during every crisis.

Another reward is narrative simplicity.

Systems are storytelling machines. They need to explain what happened to themselves and to those who oversee them. A simple narrative is valuable because it is coherent and defensible. When one person carries responsibility, the story is clear: a problem arose, a responsible person handled it, and progress continued. That narrative fits neatly into updates and reports. It is stable and easy to repeat.

Stories are also moral artifacts. They encode who did the right thing and who fell short. When a system retells an event as a story of responsibility, it is also distributing moral status. The story gives a person credit, and credit creates expectation. The next time a similar gap appears, the person who was credited becomes the person the system expects to respond. The story thus becomes a tool for stabilizing responsibility placement.

When one person carries responsibility, the story is easy to tell.

The ease of the story is a reward in itself. It reduces the cognitive load of the system. It avoids the messy complexity of shared responsibility and distributed failure. The moral frame makes the story even easier by positioning the responsible person as a kind of stabilizing force. The person is the hero of the story, and the system can tell the story without naming the gaps it contains.

"There was an issue. Someone handled it. We moved forward."

Complex explanations threaten legitimacy.

Complexity implies that the system is not in full control, and that implication is risky. It creates the possibility of critique or oversight. The moral narrative avoids that risk by assigning responsibility to a person rather than to a structure. It turns the system's dependence into a virtue story, which is more palatable than a failure analysis. The system gains legitimacy by telling a story of responsibility rather than a story of confusion.

Over-responsibility protects the system's self-image.

Self image is not only external; it is internal. A system that sees itself as competent and well managed will resist information that challenges that self perception. Over-responsibility protects the self image by plugging gaps before they are visible. It allows the system to continue to believe that its roles and processes are sufficient, because the failures are never fully visible. The moral language helps with this protection by framing the fixes as character rather than as necessity.

Self image is maintained through everyday speech. People say "we are accountable" and mean it as a statement of identity, not as a description of processes. That identity can be sincere, but it can also become a shield. The system can point to the identity in moments of critique, asserting that it is responsible because responsible people are here. The moral frame then substitutes for evidence. It reinforces the expectation that responsibility will be absorbed rather than designed.

It prevents questions like: Why was this unclear? Why did authority fail to engage? Why was escalation discouraged?

These questions are structurally destabilizing. They imply that the system failed to provide clarity, and that its formal mechanisms were inadequate. The moral frame redirects attention away from these questions and toward the person who saved the situation. The moral narrative can even cast these questions as ungrateful or disruptive. The system is spared the discomfort of self interrogation, and the person is praised for not asking.

Systems also reward emotional containment.

Emotional containment is valuable because it keeps the system from having to respond to distress. It keeps meetings calm and preserves the appearance of stability. People who absorb responsibility often absorb blame quietly. They do not make their strain visible. They accept the emotional cost as part of the moral identity they have adopted. The system rewards this by treating them as steady and dependable. The reward is respect, but respect does not remove the cost.

The social reward for containment is often increased trust, which feels like honor. Yet this trust can be another way the system avoids confronting structural limits. The contained person is trusted precisely because they do not demand change. The system can rely on that containment as a kind of emotional infrastructure, while the person bears the cost in private. The moral language treats quiet endurance as maturity, which is why the burden can continue without formal acknowledgment.

Calmness becomes a moral standard. The person who remains composed under strain is treated as an adult, while the person who expresses fatigue can be seen as less resilient. This is not usually stated outright, which is why it is so effective. The system's praise of composure and its discomfort with visible strain create a quiet rule. The rule is learned through experience, and it keeps responsibility aligned with those who can hide their distress.

People who absorb responsibility often absorb blame quietly. They do not escalate emotionally. They do not destabilize group dynamics.

This makes them socially convenient.

Convenience here is not trivial. It allows the system to maintain harmony without making structural changes. Emotional containment becomes a social virtue. The person is praised for being calm, and silence is interpreted as strength. Shame without accusation is the other side of this dynamic. When someone expresses frustration or asks for limits, the response may not be a direct reprimand, but the tone changes. The person senses the shift and learns what kind of emotion is welcome. The system does not need to accuse; it only needs to withdraw warmth.

In contrast, insisting on authority boundaries can appear disruptive.

It introduces tension. It delays action. It forces confrontation with structure.

The disruption is not only procedural; it is moral. A person who asks for authority can be seen as self protecting rather than helpful. They may be perceived as less committed, even when their request is reasonable. The moral frame turns a structural request into a character question. The system does not have to say "you are wrong." It can simply respond with less enthusiasm and more distance. That is shame without accusation, and it is effective precisely because it is subtle.

Moral language polices boundaries by attaching virtue to flexibility and attaching suspicion to insistence. The person who says "this is not mine" can be cast as rigid, and rigidity is easily framed as a moral flaw. The system does not need to argue about roles; it can simply favor the person who is more flexible. Flexibility becomes virtue, which means responsibility flows toward the most flexible, not toward the most appropriate.

As a result, systems drift toward a preference.

Not for correctness, but for smoothness.

Smoothness is a moral aesthetic. It feels like competence, maturity, and care. It is easier to praise than correctness, because correctness requires scrutiny and challenge. The system learns to prefer the person who keeps things smooth, even if that smoothness is achieved by absorbing disproportionate responsibility. The preference is not a policy. It is a pattern of reinforcement that shapes behavior over time. Moral language stabilizes the preference by making smoothness a sign of virtue.

Smoothness is also legible. It is what leaders and peers can see without digging into details. When a system runs smoothly, it appears healthy, and health is a moral signal. The person who maintains the smooth surface becomes associated with that health, even if the surface is maintained by internal strain. The moral frame then rewards the appearance, not the distribution underneath. This creates a preference for the person who can keep the surface calm, and it discourages any move that would make the underlying complexity visible.

Over time, this preference becomes cultural.

Culture also decides whose pressure matters. When a few people routinely absorb responsibility, the culture begins to treat their discomfort as background noise. The absence of disruption is read as evidence that everything is acceptable, even if the work is concentrated. Moral language then reinforces the expectation that responsible people handle pressure quietly, and the cycle hardens into a norm that feels natural rather than constructed.

New participants learn implicitly: If you fix things, you belong. If you hesitate, you are questioned.

The learning is not usually explicit. It comes through observation and small social cues. People see who is praised, who is trusted, who is invited into inner circles. They notice who is asked to do more and who is quietly ignored. The moral framing makes the pattern feel natural rather than constructed. It reads as "this is just how responsible people act." Culture is the medium that carries the moral signals without needing to name them.

The vocabulary itself is part of the teaching. Phrases like "own it" and "step up" circulate until they feel like common sense. New participants absorb the language and the expectations it carries, often without noticing the transfer. The moral words become a shared code that tells people how to belong. Because the code is moral, it is also self enforcing; people want to be the kind of person the code celebrates. The system does not need a policy when the language already does the work.

No one needs to say this out loud.

The pattern teaches itself.

The self teaching pattern is reinforced by small acts of imitation. People mirror what is praised and avoid what is quietly disapproved. The moral vocabulary becomes the rhythm of everyday work, and the rhythm sets expectations without anyone needing to issue commands. Because the reinforcement is diffuse, no single person is accountable for it. The system thus preserves the pattern while remaining unaware of its own role in maintaining it.

The teaching happens through repetition. A responsible person takes on more, receives praise, and becomes more central. A less responsive person hesitates, receives less warmth, and becomes peripheral. The system does not need to state a rule because the moral cues are enough. This is how moral language acts as a control surface. It directs behavior through recognition and omission, through the promise of belonging and the fear of distance. The control is soft but persistent.

Eventually, over-responsibility is mistaken for leadership.

Leadership becomes defined as absorbing uncertainty, not as shaping decision rights.

The confusion is understandable, because over-responsibility looks like care. The person who absorbs risk appears to be protecting others, and that appears to be leadership. But leadership in this sense is more like containment. It holds the system together by taking in the strain. The person is celebrated for doing what the system has not organized itself to do. The praise without power continues, and the person is admired without being supported.

Leadership is then equated with endurance. The person who can carry more for longer is elevated, and the elevation feels deserved because it is framed as virtue. Yet the elevation does not necessarily bring authority to change the conditions that require endurance. The person is celebrated for sacrifice, and sacrifice becomes the measure. The moral frame thus rewards the ability to absorb without changing the structure that creates the need to absorb.

This confusion is rarely corrected.

Correcting it would require the system to redefine what it admires. It would need to distinguish between responsibility as a virtue and responsibility as a structural assignment. That distinction is hard to sustain when the system benefits from the blur. The moral frame keeps the blur intact. It is easier to keep praising the absorber than to redistribute authority.

The system remains functional. The individuals become depleted.

From the outside, nothing seems broken.

External observers see only outputs and calm, not the internal redistribution of responsibility. The moral frame reinforces this because the visible story is one of capable people doing the right thing. That story is reassuring to outsiders and to the system itself. It hides the accumulation of private strain and makes the continued reliance on the same individuals appear reasonable. The system can then interpret stability as evidence that the arrangement is sound. The calm can be persuasive even when it is expensive.

That is precisely why the pattern persists.

Functionality is an appearance. The system is operating, outputs are produced, and crises are avoided. Depletion is quiet and slow. It shows up as fatigue, diminished curiosity, and a narrowing of what feels possible. Yet the moral narrative does not treat depletion as a system signal. It treats it as personal resilience. The system can continue to call on the same person because the moral frame makes it look like strength. The costs remain in the individual until they are too large to hide.

Depletion is often interpreted as a private struggle rather than a public signal. The person may withdraw, lose energy, or become less imaginative, and the system may read that as a personal shift. The moral language of responsibility makes it hard to describe depletion as systemic. The person may even feel guilt for being tired, which is another form of shame without accusation. The system continues to rely on them because the moral frame reframes exhaustion as individual weakness.

Systems do not reward over-responsibility because they are cruel.

They reward it because it works— until it doesn't.

The reward is the immediate stability that over-responsibility provides. It keeps the system moving, keeps stories simple, and keeps emotions contained. Moral language stabilizes responsibility placement by making the act of absorption seem like a personal virtue rather than a structural workaround. That stability can last a long time, which is why the pattern is so persistent. When it finally breaks, it often looks sudden, but the conditions were built slowly by years of rewarded over-responsibility and unexamined moral framing.

The effect is not that morality is false, but that its language is used as infrastructure. Responsibility is carried along the channels of praise and shame, which are soft yet binding. The system can continue to appear fair while relying on over-responsibility, because the moral framing makes the allocation feel deserved. The control surface remains in place even when individuals change, because it lives in the collective vocabulary. That is why the pattern can survive turnover and remain largely invisible.

Chapter 7

What judgment authority is not

Judgment Authority is routinely mistaken for a property of a person. The mistake is understandable because people speak, decide, and take responsibility, so the system appears to concentrate in individuals. But the chapter's purpose is to unsettle that appearance by tracing its wrongness. The negative outline is not a clever rhetorical trick. It is the only way to stay honest when the subject is a kind of legitimacy that is felt more than it is seen. When the positive definition is offered too quickly, the reader is handed something that can be carried away. That kind of portability is exactly what judgment authority resists.

A common confusion is the belief that intelligence grants the right to decide. The association runs deep. Intelligence produces swift interpretations, elegant explanations, and persuasive coherence.

These are qualities that make speech compelling and make disagreement seem naive. Yet intelligence has no inherent power to settle what is legitimate. It can show many possible outcomes and it can argue for one of them, but it cannot define which outcome the system must accept. The mind can illuminate a situation without being the source of its binding consequence.

The difference becomes visible in quiet rooms rather than dramatic ones. A junior analyst might see the risk in a plan that a senior leader missed. The analyst can articulate it, document it, and defend it. The words can be right, the reasoning immaculate, and the probabilities aligned. Still the decision moves as if the analysis were a suggestion rather than a boundary. The reasoning does not fail. The authority is simply elsewhere. The situation makes clear that intelligence can be present and even decisive in substance while still being irrelevant in legitimacy.

The inverse is equally revealing. A person can have the formal ability to decide while clearly lacking in intelligence as conventionally measured. Systems tolerate this not because they are blind to quality, but because their primary need is order. A decision that arrives from the designated place is often preferred to a better decision that arrives from an illegitimate place. This is not a defense of poor judgment. It is a description of how legitimacy works in practice. Intelligence makes a decision better or worse. It does not make it authoritative.

The misalignment persists because intelligence is difficult to verify, and authority is designed to be seen. In a group, intelligence is inferred through performance: quickness of speech, technical vocabulary, calmness under pressure. These are signals, not guarantees. They can be accurate. They can also be faked. The group then assumes authority where it recognizes intelligence, not because the intelligence truly confers authority, but because the group needs a shortcut. The shortcut is attractive. It is also fragile.

The fragility appears when the subject matter shifts. A person regarded as brilliant in one area can be treated as broadly authoritative, even when the subject moves to a place where their brilliance is irrelevant. The assumption of transfer is seductive because it feels efficient. It also produces the same confusion repeatedly: a person who is excellent at diagnosing technical flaws is treated as the natural decider in a dispute about values, risk tolerance, or timing. The authority seems to follow the person, but it only follows the symbol of their intelligence.

Experience is another proxy that often masquerades as authority. Time in a system suggests accumulated knowledge, and accumulated knowledge suggests the right to decide. But experience is not the same as legitimacy. It is memory, sometimes practical, sometimes nostalgic, sometimes distorted by survival. A person can have decades of exposure to a process and still have no recognized capacity to define its outcomes. Another person can arrive without memory and be placed into the position of final judgment. The system may appear irrational from the outside, yet it is operating on a different logic than personal credibility.

Experience can even mislead the people who possess it. Repetition produces patterns, and patterns can become assumptions. The person who has seen the same decision go one way ten times begins to regard that path as natural, not because it is legitimate, but because it is familiar. When the environment changes, the experience becomes a filter that rejects new evidence. The individual then asserts authority by invoking memory, and the invocation is treated as if it were itself a source of legitimacy. It is not. It is an argument from habit.

Long tenure often creates a social economy of deference. People speak differently to those who have been present for years. They ask permission, they ask for context, they ask for stories. The deference can look like respect for authority, but it is often respect for endurance. The person who stayed has seen others depart. That endurance can carry moral weight, even when it carries no structural right to define outcomes. The person may feel the weight as a burden. The group may treat it as a mandate. Both perceptions can be sincere, and both can be wrong about legitimacy.

Experience also travels poorly. The boundaries that make a decision binding in one institution do not necessarily exist in another. A veteran public official can move into a private organization and find that a lifetime of experience does not automatically translate into authority. Conversely, an executive can move into a public institution and be surrounded by rituals of authority that feel empty. The confusion is not a personal failure. It is an instance of a deeper fact: experience is information about the past, while authority is a present arrangement of recognition.

Confidence is perhaps the most theatrical proxy. It creates the illusion of certainty in uncertain conditions. It places a tone around an idea and makes that tone sound like inevitability. Groups often surrender to the confident voice because hesitation feels like weakness and weakness feels like danger. Yet confidence can be completely detached from legitimate authority. It can be a performance, a coping mechanism, or a social strategy. It can also be genuine, but authenticity does not transform it into a mandate.

Confidence is also contagious. It relieves anxiety, and in doing so it gathers followers. That following can be mistaken for authority because it looks like consent. It is not. A crowd can agree and still be wrong about what is recognized as binding within the system. The person at the center of that crowd can feel empowered and still have no structural capacity to make the decision stick. When the crowd disperses, the decision evaporates. The confidence remains a memory of a moment rather than a durable change in reality.

The effect is pronounced in meetings. The person who speaks with certainty, who finishes sentences without interruption, who offers a conclusion without visible doubt, often becomes the unofficial decider. Others adjust their speech accordingly. They frame their input as contribution rather than challenge. The room moves. But the movement is not necessarily authority. It is momentum, and momentum can die at the door of the person who actually holds the recognized right to decide. The confident speaker may then appear to have been overruled, when in fact they never had authority to begin with.

Competence is another frequent confusion. Competence is demonstrated capacity. It is the ability to do the work and see the consequences. When competence is visible, it feels reasonable to cede authority. The ceding can be appropriate, but it is not automatic. A competent person can be required to execute decisions they did not choose. They can be trusted to deliver, and still be excluded from the legitimacy of definition. This is not an insult to their competence. It is a separation of function.

The separation is often painful because it contradicts a deeply held belief about fairness. If someone knows the situation best, it feels natural that they should decide. The dissonance between that belief and actual institutional arrangements becomes a source of cynicism. People then misread authority as a personal betrayal, when it is often a structural constraint. The personal feeling is real, but it does not change the arrangement. It only exposes the emotional cost of assuming competence is a ticket to authority.

Responsibility is another condition that feels adjacent but is not the same. Responsibility names who will be affected, who will be blamed, who will absorb the consequences. Authority names who can establish the meaning of those consequences. A person can be responsible without being authorized. They can suffer the effects of a decision they did not control. A person can be authorized without bearing the most direct consequences. Both positions feel wrong to the person in them. The misalignment is common enough that it begins to appear normal.

The effect of this misalignment is subtle. It changes how people speak about failure. They begin to describe outcomes as if they were inevitable, because admitting that a decision was imposed reveals their lack of authority. The language becomes defensive or fatalistic. The environment learns to treat accountability as personal burden rather than structural location. Over time, the distance between responsibility and authority becomes a chronic source of resentment. The resentment can be loud or silent. Either way, it does not change legitimacy.

Power is also not the same as judgment authority. Power can force an outcome. It can punish, reward, or intimidate. It can compel compliance. But a compelled outcome is not necessarily legitimate. It can be reversed the moment the force is removed. It can be ignored when circumstances shift. Authority does not require brute force. It requires recognition. The distinction matters because systems often confuse stability with legitimacy. A stable outcome produced by force may appear authoritative, but it remains unstable underneath, like a dam held by constant pressure.

Power can also be temporary and situational. A person with access to resources can shape outcomes even without recognized authority. They can make things happen and create the impression that they have the right to make them happen. Yet their influence is contingent on access, not on legitimacy. When access changes, the authority dissolves. The system never truly recognized the person as the place where decisions become binding. It merely tolerated the effects of their power.

Symbolic authority complicates all of these confusions. Symbols are efficient. They allow a group to coordinate without constantly renegotiating legitimacy. A title, a uniform, a credential, a ritual, even a seat at a table, can stand in for the invisible structure that actually confers authority. The symbol is not the authority, but it is designed to point toward it. The problem is that symbols are portable and authority is not. The symbol can travel into contexts where the structure does not follow, and the deference will often follow the symbol anyway.

This is why former leaders retain an aura even after their formal authority has ended. The language around them changes, the meetings change, and people continue to treat their opinions as decisions. The inertia is understandable. Symbols train people to recognize authority quickly. When the symbol persists, the recognition persists, even if the legitimacy has expired. The confusion is not just psychological; it can become organizational. Decisions may drift toward the person who no longer holds the right to define them, creating informal authority that is never properly acknowledged.

The reverse also happens. A person who is newly appointed to a role can carry the formal authority of the position but lack the symbolic cues that would make others recognize it. The title on paper is not enough. The group watches for the symbols it expects, and in their absence it treats the authority as provisional. The new authority can feel strangely powerless even when it is legitimate, because recognition has not caught up. This gap can persist for a long time. It is not always resolved by performance, because performance is not itself a symbol of legitimacy.

Credentials are another form of symbol. They compress years of study into a visual marker, a line of text, an abbreviation. They are often valuable and often earned. Yet they are not authority. A credential can invite deference, but it does not define what is binding in a particular system. A credential can be irrelevant to the decision at hand, or it can be insufficient in a setting where authority is assigned by role rather than expertise. People may still defer because they lack their own criteria for legitimacy, but the deference is a social choice, not an institutional rule.

Rituals similarly create the appearance of authority. The formal meeting, the agenda, the sequence of voices, the recorded minutes, the signature, the ceremonial announcement—these do not create authority, but they make it visible. The ritual is sometimes mistaken for the decision itself. A decision can be made informally and then retroactively inserted into the ritual. A decision can be made formally and still lack legitimacy if it was not authorized by the system's actual structure. The ritual is a wrapper. The authority is the content, and the two are not identical.

Even language can function as a symbol. Certain phrases signal finality, certain terms signal jurisdiction. People learn to hear those signals and respond to them. The language of authority can be learned and imitated. An imitation can be persuasive enough to make others comply. But it is still imitation. The legitimacy of judgment is not a rhetorical achievement. The rhetorical effect can be useful, but it cannot alter who is recognized as having the right to decide. The system may tolerate the performance for a while, but tolerance is not recognition.

Expertise is perhaps the most treacherous symbol because it is both real and misleading. Expertise is real in the sense that it reflects deep knowledge and skill. It is misleading because it creates a halo that is not bounded by the domain where it was earned. A person known for expertise in one field is invited to opine on adjacent questions, then on distant ones, and the invitations begin to sound like authority. The expert's opinion becomes a default. The group assumes legitimacy has transferred, even though the structure has not changed.

The illusion is intensified by asymmetry. When someone else lacks the knowledge to evaluate the expert's reasoning, they treat the reasoning as authority. The expert becomes a kind of oracle. The group then confuses inability to evaluate with recognition. They accept the expert's conclusion because they cannot judge it, not because they have decided that the expert has the right to decide. The consent is a substitute for understanding, and the substitution is necessary at times. But it is not the same as authority.

Institutional expertise can also hide the boundary between advice and judgment. A research group can produce a recommendation that is technically impeccable. The recommendation can become policy because it is convenient, not because the group has the authority to decide. The distinction is subtle and easily lost. When the policy is challenged, the group may discover that it had influence but not legitimacy. The people who treated the recommendation as binding may then feel betrayed, even though the authority never truly resided there.

The same confusion appears in professional services. Consultants, auditors, specialists, and experts often wield influence that feels like authority. Their reports, diagnoses, or assessments can shape a decision. Yet their role is advisory unless the structure explicitly grants more. The advice can be decisive in practice, but that is still not authority. The system can ignore it without violating its own rules. The distinction matters because when things go wrong, the responsibility falls elsewhere, and the expert discovers that influence and authority are not the same kind of power.

Another source of illusion is proximity to decision makers. People who sit near authority, who speak often with those who hold it, or who are seen walking with them, acquire a reflected legitimacy. Others treat them as extensions of authority. They begin to act as if their statements are binding. Sometimes they are. Often they are not. The difference is known only to those inside the structure. To everyone else, the difference appears as subtle shifts in tone and timing, which are easy to misread.

Visibility also distorts perception. Those who speak publicly, who publish, or who are quoted are treated as authoritative, not because the system granted them legitimacy, but because they are the most visible. Public visibility becomes a proxy. Yet visibility is an accident of media and attention, not a marker of legitimate judgment. The public may follow a visible figure's conclusions, and organizations may even respond as if those conclusions were binding, but that is responsiveness, not authority.

The confusion between authority and persuasion is persistent. Persuasion changes minds. Authority changes the recognized state of things. A persuasive argument can lead to a decision, but it can also fail to do so without violating any rule. Authority can make a decision stick even when it persuades no one. The distinction is uncomfortable because it reveals that legitimacy can be disconnected from agreement. That discomfort often leads people to treat persuasion as if it were authority, because the alternative feels undemocratic or unfair. The feeling does not change the structure.

The social appetite for fairness is one reason these confusions are so resilient. People want the best argument to win, the most experienced person to be heard, the most competent person to decide. Those desires are not naive; they are ethical aspirations. But they are aspirations, not descriptions. When the structure assigns authority elsewhere, the aspirations become disappointed. The disappointment is then projected onto individuals as if they were responsible for the structural arrangement. The projection obscures the underlying reality and keeps the confusion alive.

Another reason is psychological. It is easier to believe that authority comes from personal qualities because those qualities feel accessible. If authority can be earned by intelligence, experience, or confidence, then it is within reach. If authority is a structural recognition, then it is not fully in one's control. The negative definition threatens the sense of agency. That threat creates resistance, which in turn produces stronger attachment to the proxies. The attachment is not irrational. It is a response to a deeper discomfort.

This is why the language of merit and the language of authority often blur together. Merit describes deserving. Authority describes legitimacy. In a healthy system they are aligned often enough to keep the system functional. But they are not the same, and their alignment is contingent. When people see merit without authority, they feel the system is unjust. When they see authority without merit, they feel it is corrupted. Both reactions can be true, and neither reaction automatically changes the structure. The judgments remain personal. The authority remains elsewhere.

The confusion is particularly acute when authority is distributed. In collaborative settings, people are told that decisions are made together. The rhetoric of collaboration suggests shared authority.

Yet the recognition of legitimacy is often asymmetric. Some voices carry final weight, even if that weight is not acknowledged. Others are invited in, yet their role remains advisory. The tension between rhetoric and reality makes it hard to see where authority truly sits. People then infer it from personality, expertise, or persistence, and the proxies fill the void.

That void is also filled by process. When a system is ambiguous, its procedures become the apparent source of legitimacy. The process is treated as if it were the authority, because it is the only visible thing that can be pointed to. Yet process is a container, not a source. A process can be followed without any authority behind it, and authority can be exercised without strict adherence to process. The process can provide comfort, but it does not create legitimacy on its own.

The reliance on process creates another illusion: that whoever runs the process holds authority. Facilitators, coordinators, and administrators can appear to be the decision makers because they manage the ritual. In reality, they often carry no such legitimacy. They are conduits for the authority of others. Their role is crucial, but it is not the same as judgment authority. Treating it as such can create unexpected friction when their guidance is treated as a decision rather than a channel.

The chapter's negative approach is also meant to resist another common confusion: the belief that authority can be deduced from the correctness of a decision. When a decision proves correct in hindsight, people retroactively treat the decider as if they had authority all along. The success creates legitimacy after the fact. The reverse happens with failure. A decision that fails is treated as if it must have been illegitimate, even if it was authorized. This retroactive rewriting of legitimacy makes authority seem like a property of outcomes, when it is actually a property of recognition at the moment of decision.

Legitimacy is not the same as popularity. A popular decision can still be illegitimate, and an unpopular one can be authorized. Popularity feels like consent, and consent feels like authority, but the two are not the same. The system may value popularity, but it is still a preference, not a rule. When popularity is mistaken for authority, the group is shocked by the persistence of an unpopular decision. They then frame the persistence as stubbornness rather than structure. The surprise reveals the confusion.

A similar confusion occurs with transparency. A transparent process feels legitimate. People can see what happened, so they assume it is authorized. Transparency is valuable, but it does not generate authority. A transparent decision can still be illegitimate if it was made by someone without the recognized right to decide. An opaque decision can still be legitimate if it came from the recognized source. The human appetite for visibility makes transparency feel like legitimacy, and that feeling often overrides careful analysis of where authority actually sits.

The dynamics of authority also shift with scale. In small groups, authority feels personal because the recognition flows through relationships. In large systems, authority feels abstract because the recognition is embedded in rules, roles, and procedures. The two extremes are not different kinds of authority; they are different presentations. The personal presentation makes it easier to confuse authority with personality. The abstract presentation makes it easier to confuse authority with process. Both confusions are common because both presentations hide the same underlying recognition.

Crisis conditions intensify the confusion. When time is scarce, groups seek clarity. The person who appears decisive can be elevated to authority even if no structural recognition exists. The elevation can be necessary for action, but it is not the same as legitimate judgment. After the crisis, the temporary authority may linger, and the group may retroactively treat it as if it had been legitimate all along. The memory of crisis becomes a myth of authority, and the myth can outlive the actual structure that allowed it.

Symbolic authority becomes especially powerful in crisis. Uniforms, insignia, titles, and command language provide a sense of order. They are valued because they offer a narrative of control. Yet they can also displace the actual structure of legitimacy. A person who looks like authority can be treated as authority, while the person who is authorized but not visibly so is ignored. The crisis intensifies the reliance on symbols, which intensifies the risk of confusion.

The attachment to proxies has another cost: it can make the holder of authority invisible to themselves. A person in a role of authority may be convinced that their legitimacy rests on intelligence, experience, or confidence. They may work hard to maintain those qualities, believing that any lapse will dissolve their authority. The effort can be exhausting and unnecessary. Authority, when it exists, does not require constant performance. But the confusion makes the performance feel essential, and the person becomes trapped in an endless display.

The people around them also suffer. If authority is mistaken for intelligence, then those who disagree with the authorized person will be treated as foolish. If authority is mistaken for experience, then those who lack tenure will be treated as naive. If authority is mistaken for confidence, then those who speak cautiously will be dismissed. The proxies then become tools of social exclusion. The exclusion is justified by a false definition of authority, and the group loses access to valuable perspectives without acknowledging the structural choice it has made.

There is another subtle error: the belief that authority is equivalent to ownership. Ownership can carry authority, but it does not always. In some settings, ownership grants the right to decide. In others, ownership is separate from governance. People assume that the person who pays is the person who defines. This assumption can be true in one environment and false in another. The assumption persists because it is simple. But it is only a proxy. Legitimacy depends on recognition within the particular system, not on a universal rule about ownership.

Legal authority is often invoked as a stabilizing concept, but legal form is still not identical to judgment authority. Law can define boundaries of legitimacy, yet within those boundaries the actual recognition can still be contested. A decision can be legal and still be treated as illegitimate by the people subject to it. The inverse can also happen. A decision can be widely accepted and still be legally unauthorized. The tension between legal form and social recognition reveals the layered nature of legitimacy. The layers do not always align.

Another illusion is the belief that authority is always explicit. People search for a document, a policy, or a clear statement. When they cannot find it, they infer that no authority exists. But authority can be implicit, woven into habits, defaults, and expectations. It can be recognized through practice without being written down. This makes it difficult to challenge because there is nothing explicit to argue with. Yet the implicit nature does not make it less real. It merely makes it harder to see, and that invisibility fuels the dependence on proxies.

The idea that authority is always stable is also false. It can change, shift, and decay. The recognition that grants legitimacy can erode without any formal announcement. A person who once held unquestioned authority can lose it slowly, through accumulated decisions, changes in context, or shifts in institutional priorities. They may still carry the symbols of authority, and they may still speak with confidence. The system's recognition, however, may have moved elsewhere. The person then experiences the disorienting sensation of still being listened to, but no longer being obeyed.

This decay is often misinterpreted as a personal failure. The person believes their intelligence has faded, their experience has become irrelevant, their confidence has been noticed as empty. These explanations are appealing because they are personal and actionable. Yet the deeper change may be structural: a reorganization, a shift in ownership, a new regulatory constraint, a silent change in who signs and who approves. The person perceives the loss of authority as a loss of self, when it is often a change in recognition.

The negative definition also clarifies why disagreements can persist even when all parties are competent and well intentioned. If authority is located in the wrong place, the correctness of arguments is irrelevant. People can spend hours refining their reasoning, gathering evidence, and articulating their positions, only to be overridden by a single decision from the authorized place. The effort feels wasted because it was. The problem was never the quality of the argument. The problem was that authority was elsewhere, and no amount of reasoning could relocate it.

This is why debates about merit often fail to resolve conflicts about authority. Merit can decide what is best. Authority decides what is binding. When the two diverge, the debate becomes a moral argument about fairness rather than a recognition of structure. The moral argument can be important, but it does not, by itself, alter legitimacy. People then feel powerless and conclude that the system is corrupt, when in reality the system is functioning as designed. The recognition may be unjust, but it is still recognition.

The place where this is most visible is in institutions that carry both mission and hierarchy. The mission suggests that the most morally aligned person should decide. The hierarchy assigns that right differently. When the two conflict, people feel betrayed by the institution. They then attempt to claim authority through moral superiority, through dedication, through sacrifice. These are powerful signals, but they do not create legitimacy unless the structure acknowledges them. The person may be admirable and still unauthorized.

This brings the discussion back to the core proxies. Intelligence is compelling because it promises correctness. Experience is compelling because it promises wisdom. Confidence is compelling because it promises stability. None of these promises are the same as legitimacy. The system can value them, and often does. But it uses them as input, not as the source of recognition. The negative definition makes room for that complexity without pretending that virtue or skill alone defines authority.

Another area where the confusion is persistent is in the language of representation. Representatives are often treated as if their personal judgment authority is elevated by virtue of representing others. Representation, however, is a mechanism, not a source. It can delegate authority, but only within the limits set by the system that created the representation. The representative can feel empowered and still be constrained. The represented group can feel betrayed and still have no direct authority. The legitimacy remains in the structure that defined representation in the first place.

The same confusion appears in the relationship between founders and their organizations. Founders are often treated as if their authority is intrinsic, because they created the entity. Yet creation does not necessarily confer perpetual legitimacy. As organizations evolve, authority can be redistributed, formalized, or constrained. The founder may retain symbols of authority long after the structure has shifted. The group may continue to defer out of gratitude or myth. The authority can thus appear personal when it is actually a negotiated recognition that has changed over time.

Narrative also plays a role. People tell stories about who is decisive, who is visionary, who is the source of the organization's success. These stories attach authority to individuals in a way that can survive changes in structure. The narrative provides continuity, but it can also distort current legitimacy. The story of a past decision can be used to justify present authority, even if the person no longer holds it. In this way narrative becomes a symbolic proxy, and the proxy can outrun reality.

The emphasis on negative definition is a safeguard against those narratives. It prevents the reader from collapsing authority into personal myth. It insists that the admired qualities of a person, or the persuasive power of their story, are not sufficient to define legitimacy.

The admired qualities may make a person influential. The story may make their words persuasive. Neither automatically makes their decisions binding. The binding force comes from recognition, and recognition is a property of the system, not of the individual story.

Another illusion arises when authority is conflated with accountability mechanisms. If a person is held accountable, it can look like they have authority. In practice, accountability can be assigned to those who do not decide, precisely because their lack of authority makes them safer to blame. The blame travels downward because it is politically convenient, not because it reflects legitimate decision making. The people at the top may be shielded, and those lower may be exposed. The misalignment then becomes normalized as the ordinary cost of participation.

This normalization leads people to internalize blame as if it were a personal failure. They assume they must have failed to persuade, failed to prove competence, failed to demonstrate confidence. They then attempt to compensate by increasing those proxies, hoping that authority will follow. The effort can improve their influence, and it can improve outcomes, but it does not guarantee legitimacy. The structure remains intact, and the person remains outside of it. The negative definition is meant to relieve the confusion, not to console it.

There is a further complication: authority can be recognized without being explicit, and it can be explicit without being recognized. In some cultures and organizations, authority is communicated through subtle cues and interpersonal deference rather than formal declarations. A person can hold a title yet find that their decisions do not stick because the informal recognition is elsewhere. Another person can hold no title and still be treated as the person whose judgment defines what happens next. These situations are often dismissed as political, but they are also a reminder that authority is a collective recognition, not a personal possession.

The gap between formal and informal recognition creates a fertile ground for misunderstanding. People who rely on formal symbols feel undermined. People who rely on informal networks feel accused of illegitimacy. The conflict becomes personal, yet the real issue is the mismatch between symbols and recognition. The negative definition refuses to grant either side the comfort of a simple answer. It insists that authority cannot be identified by title alone, or by influence alone, or by moral argument alone. It is a relationship between structure and acknowledgment.

Another misconception is that authority is always consciously granted. People often imagine a clear moment of authorization, a decision that names the authorized person. In practice, recognition can emerge through repeated patterns. The group discovers who is listened to, who can settle disputes, who can direct resources without challenge. The recognition becomes a habit. Yet a habit can also conceal the fact that authority is being exercised without explicit mandate. People then treat the habit as a fact of nature, and the authority becomes invisible and unquestioned.

When that happens, authority can be exercised without accountability, because no one has named it. The person who holds it may not even recognize it in themselves. They simply notice that their statements become outcomes. The group notices the same and adjusts. The recognition is diffuse and therefore difficult to contest. The lack of explicitness makes it appear as if authority is absent, when in fact it has merely become embedded. The proxies then become even more tempting, because they offer a visible explanation for what is otherwise hidden.

The chapter's focus on what authority is not is also a response to the temptation to reduce it to a moral hierarchy. It is easy to treat authority as a reward for virtue. It feels just to imagine that the most ethical, selfless, or principled person should decide. In some settings, that aspiration is incorporated into how authority is assigned. In many settings, it is not. The system may reward traits unrelated to virtue, and it may penalize moral courage. The mismatch can feel like a betrayal of ideals, but ideals are not authority.

The belief that authority is moral can also be weaponized. People can claim authority by claiming virtue. They can frame disagreement as immorality, and through that frame they seek to make their judgments binding. The move is persuasive, and it can be powerful, but it is still a substitute for recognition. The group may comply out of fear or shame rather than because the system recognizes the claim. The compliance may then be temporary or unstable. The moral language does not create authority; it creates pressure.

The negative definition therefore has a protective function. It prevents the reader from confusing the force of moral conviction with the force of legitimate judgment. It also prevents the reader from mistaking the clarity of a well-argued position for the right to decide. It keeps the attention on structure and recognition, even though those are less satisfying than personal virtue or intellectual brilliance. The refusal to provide a positive definition is not a refusal to explain. It is a refusal to make the phenomenon portable in a way that would mislead.

The discussion of false proxies also clarifies why the experience of authority is often alienating. Those who do not hold it can feel invisible, even when they are competent. Those who do hold it can feel isolated, even when they are confident. The reasons for these feelings are not always personal. They are often structural. But the proxies encourage people to interpret the feelings in personal terms. The competent person assumes they lack intelligence. The confident person assumes they have failed to inspire. The interpretations are wrong in different ways, and the confusion persists.

The alienation is compounded by the way authority narrows perception. When authority is held, the range of signals that matter shifts. People begin to filter information based on what will be recognized by the system. They begin to treat some voices as noise and others as necessary. This is not a moral failing. It is a consequence of the role. Yet the person inside the role may experience the narrowing as a loss of authenticity. They may then seek to compensate by performing empathy or openness, which are again proxies rather than sources of legitimacy.

The person outside the role experiences a different distortion. They see the authority as arbitrary because they do not see the recognition that sustains it. They conclude that the authority must rest on personal qualities or on corruption. They then respond by trying to improve those personal qualities or by trying to expose corruption. These responses can be rational, but they may miss the structure. The structure is indifferent to personal improvement and resilient to exposure. It responds to recognition, not to argument.

The negative definition also makes room for the uncomfortable truth that authority can be granted for reasons that are not admirable. It can be granted for speed, for convenience, for political compromise, for historical accident. None of these reasons are attractive as foundations for legitimacy. Yet they can be sufficient. The authority that results may feel undeserved or unjust, but it still holds. To call it illegitimate is to make a moral argument, not to change the recognition. The system remains intact until the recognition shifts.

At the same time, the negative definition avoids the cynical trap that authority is always arbitrary. The fact that authority is not intelligence, not experience, and not confidence does not mean it is random. It means that its source is not personal virtue or skill. The source is recognition embedded in structure. That recognition can be stable and coherent even if it is not admirable. The chapter's purpose is not to celebrate or condemn, but to clarify what authority is not, so that the reader can stop chasing its shadows.

This clarity also reveals why authority often feels invisible to those who do not hold it. From their perspective, decisions appear to emerge from discussion, persuasion, or conflict. They do not see the moment when recognition converts a judgment into a binding outcome. That moment may occur in a private conversation, in an approval chain, or in a tacit expectation. The invisibility makes it easy to confuse authority with whatever is visible: eloquence, tenure, confidence, charisma. The negative definition interrupts that reflex.

The invisibility is not always accidental. Some systems benefit from keeping authority ambiguous because ambiguity reduces direct challenge. If authority is unclear, dissent can be contained, and responsibility can be distributed downward. The ambiguity also allows symbolic proxies to operate more freely. People argue about who is smartest or most experienced rather than about who is authorized. The argument stays at the level of personal qualities, which is safer for the structure. The structure remains intact, largely unexamined.

The absence of a positive definition can feel frustrating, and that frustration is part of the point. When a concept refuses to become a checklist or a recipe, it forces attention to the environment rather than the individual. The reader may want a pathway, a method, a framework. The chapter declines to provide it because any such pathway would imply that authority can be manufactured through personal effort. That implication would be false. Authority can be sought, negotiated, and recognized, but those actions depend on context and structure, not on a universal model.

The consequences of this misunderstanding are practical as well as psychological. Organizations that conflate authority with intelligence may promote brilliant individuals into roles where their brilliance is irrelevant, and then wonder why decisions become unstable. Organizations that conflate authority with experience may entrench habits and call them wisdom, then struggle to adapt. Organizations that conflate authority with confidence may reward performance over substance, then discover that confidence cannot substitute for legitimacy when conditions change. These are not moral failings. They are structural confusions with real costs.

The confusions also shape how dissent is managed. When authority is conflated with confidence, dissenters who speak cautiously are dismissed. When authority is conflated with experience, dissenters who lack tenure are ignored. When authority is conflated with intelligence, dissenters who do not perform brilliance are sidelined. The system then narrows its own range of information, not because it intends to, but because it has mistaken proxies for legitimacy. The narrowing can appear as consensus, but it is often just exclusion.

The negative definition of authority therefore has a diagnostic effect. It allows the reader to see the places where their own assumptions about intelligence, experience, and confidence are doing the work that recognition should be doing. It does not provide a substitute. It does not say where authority truly lies. It only says that if you are using those proxies as the answer, you are almost certainly looking in the wrong place. The absence of a positive definition is a refusal to replace one proxy with another.

That refusal is important because the subject invites metaphor. Authority is tempting to describe as gravity, as weight, as a center. Those metaphors create the impression that authority is a natural force rather than a social recognition. They make it feel inevitable, and they make it feel personal. The chapter uses negative definition to resist the metaphorical drift. It keeps the focus on what authority is not, which keeps the reader from turning it into an object with simple properties.

In practice, the person who holds authority often appears unremarkable. They may not be the most intelligent or the most experienced. They may lack confidence. They may be disliked. Yet their decisions are binding. The appearance of ordinariness is not a paradox. It is a sign that authority is not a personal trait. The person is a carrier of recognition, not its source. This does not make their character irrelevant. It makes their character insufficient to explain legitimacy.

The negative definition also helps explain why authority can be so frustrating to contest. If it were intelligence, then an argument could beat it. If it were experience, then evidence could unseat it. If it were confidence, then a stronger performance could replace it. But authority is none of those, so none of those tactics are guaranteed to work. The person who tries them may feel gaslit when they fail.

The failure is not a trick. It is a mismatch between the tool and the structure.

This mismatch is what creates the sense of futility that sometimes surrounds decision making. People feel as if they are participating in a process, yet the outcome seems predetermined. They then attribute the outcome to hidden intelligence, hidden experience, or hidden confidence. The hiddenness becomes a conspiracy in their minds. The reality is often simpler: authority is recognized elsewhere, and the visible process is not the source of the binding decision. The negative definition strips away the conspiracy and leaves the structure exposed.

There is no attempt here to deny the value of intelligence, experience, or confidence. They are valuable in their own domains. They make judgments better, they make actions more effective, they make communication more efficient. The claim is only that they do not create legitimate authority. Treating them as the source of legitimacy creates a chain of misunderstanding that leads to wasted effort, misplaced blame, and distorted expectations. The negative definition aims to halt that chain by clarifying the limits.

The absence of a positive definition is also a protection against the temptation to romanticize authority. People often imagine that authority confers clarity, peace, or control. The person with authority is imagined to be certain, wise, and calm. In reality, authority often intensifies uncertainty because it exposes the consequences of judgment. The person can be uncertain and still authorized. The authority does not dissolve ambiguity. It merely gives someone the right to declare which ambiguity will be acted upon. To romanticize authority is to confuse it with confidence or wisdom, which are again proxies.

When the reader reaches the end of this chapter, the concept should feel clearer, but not portable. It should feel like a boundary drawn around what authority is not, rather than a recipe for how to obtain it. The point is not to grant authority or to show how it can be seized. The point is to remove the false comfort of proxies. Once they are removed, the remaining shape is not a tool. It is a recognition that authority is a structural phenomenon that cannot be reduced to personal qualities.

That recognition is not meant to be empowering or disempowering. It is meant to be accurate. The reader might feel a sense of loss, because the proxies are familiar and reassuring. They make authority feel earned and attainable. The negative definition denies that reassurance. It insists that legitimacy is not a reward for intelligence, experience, or confidence. It is a different kind of fact. To see that fact is to see the limits of personal agency in systems, and that is a different kind of understanding.

The chapter ends where it began: judgment authority is not intelligence, not experience, and not confidence. It is not competence, not responsibility, not power, not popularity, not transparency, not process, not virtue, not narrative, and not symbol. These are not trivial distinctions. They are the difference between understanding why a decision becomes binding and assuming that it does. The negative definition is therefore not a retreat from explanation. It is the most faithful explanation that can be offered without turning authority into a transferable method.

Chapter 8

How the absence of authority disguises itself

When judgment authority is absent, it rarely appears as absence.

It disguises itself.

The absence is rarely announced because absence destabilizes. People need a story about where decisions go. A system that openly admits that no one decides invites confusion, resistance, or exit. So the gap is covered with forms that look like decision. The forms can be gentle or formal, but they are still coverings.

A disguise also protects the people inside it. If authority is absent, the person who notices the absence becomes exposed. They are left holding recognition without a place to put it. The disguise offers a place, even if that place does not carry authority. It turns raw recognition into something that feels socially acceptable, something that can be spoken without demanding consequence.

In that sense, the disguise does not erase recognition. It regulates it. It channels recognition into rituals that are safe, into conversations that cannot compel, into acknowledgments that remain reversible.

Visibility is a key part of this regulation. When recognition is displayed, it appears to have been handled. The system can point to the display as proof of responsiveness, even if the display does not connect to authority. Visibility becomes a substitute for consequence.

This is why the artifacts of recognition matter so much. Documents and dashboards, public statements and listening sessions, carefully phrased summaries that show the system has heard. These artifacts can be useful. They can capture nuance and preserve memory. They can also become the evidence that replaces action. The existence of a record is treated as a form of closure.

The display creates a shared reference, which feels like collective ownership. People can point to the record and say, This is what we know.That knowledge is real, but ownership is not control. The record can be respected without being empowered.

Recognition then becomes partly performative. Not in the sense of insincerity, but in the sense that it must be shaped to fit the available form. People learn what counts as a valid contribution. They learn the language that travels. The disguise is reinforced because the performance feels like participation, and participation feels like authority.

The disguise is not only visual. It is structural. It changes how recognition feels. It takes the human capacity to notice, to describe, to interpret, and it places that capacity inside rooms where notice does not obligate response. Recognition remains intact, but the link between recognition and action is severed.

The severing is rarely named. It is felt in the small frictions of daily life, in the sense that a clear observation lands softly and then disappears. When recognition is vivid, it creates an expectation of movement. That expectation is a cultural habit, not a structural law. The disguise survives by letting the habit do the work.

This separation is difficult to perceive from the inside. Modern settings tend to treat recognition as a kind of pressure. If something is seen clearly, then surely something will happen. The social imagination is full of this expectation. The expectation is not always stated, but it is present in the small signals of conversation, in the tempo of meetings, in the little nods that sound like alignment.

Many people learn early that noticing carries responsibility. The child who points out a mess is expected to help clean it. The colleague who spots a risk is expected to mitigate it. The ethic becomes implicit: recognition is the first step toward action. This ethic is socially useful in many contexts, but it becomes misleading when authority is absent. The person feels compelled to move, while the structure provides no path for movement.

When authority is absent, recognition still happens. People still see. They still articulate. They still care. What disappears is the obligation to move. That is the quiet center of the disguise.

The absence of obligation produces a peculiar kind of stillness. Stillness is not nothing. It is active restraint, a lack of permission, a holding pattern that can be full of meaning. But in a culture that equates care with action, stillness is experienced as awkward. It feels like a gap between the heart and the hands. The disguise manages this discomfort by substituting activity for authority, so the system appears responsive even when it cannot be changed.

Most systems do not tell you: "You are not allowed to decide."

Instead, they offer substitutes.

The substitutes are often reassuring. They allow the system to appear open without becoming vulnerable. They let people feel that their recognition matters, which keeps participation alive. They give the system a way to absorb attention without yielding control. Substitutes are socially efficient. They create the appearance of responsibility without the consequences of responsibility.

The substitutes are often very close to judgment. They share the language of deliberation. They share the feelings of seriousness. They borrow the intimacy of decision without carrying its weight. This closeness is what makes the disguise stable. If the substitute felt nothing like judgment, people would refuse it. If it felt exactly like judgment, it would be judgment. The system stays functional by holding that narrow middle ground, where the form is preserved and the consequence is withheld.

The form can be meticulous. It can involve minutes, summaries, action items, and recorded outcomes. It can be staffed by thoughtful people. It can include data, stories, and emotional testimony. The presence of these elements makes the substitute convincing. They are not fake. They are simply decoupled from binding authority.

In such spaces, recognition can be present for long periods without becoming action. In fact, recognition can be rewarded precisely because it does not force change. A system can be praised for listening, for holding forums, for collecting insights, without actually altering its path. This is a form of social insulation. It allows the system to absorb awareness while preserving its current shape.

Social insulation can look like maturity. The system appears to be processing. It appears to be holding complexity. It appears to be resisting rash moves. Those appearances are not wrong, but they are not the same as authority. A system can process indefinitely. It can build an archive of recognition, a detailed ledger of what people know, without any requirement to act on that ledger.

They offer discussion.

Discussion is the most elegant substitute. It feels like the mind of the system is open. It creates a shared atmosphere of seriousness. People speak in full sentences. They acknowledge each other. They refine their observations. Discussion does not require a decision to exist. It only requires attention.

Discussion also creates a sense of shared temporality. People can return to the same topic again and again, feeling that each round brings deeper understanding. That depth can be real. It can also become a way to keep recognition in motion without giving it a destination. Conversation becomes a holding pattern, not because anyone intends it, but because no one has the authority to end it.

In many cultures, attention is treated as a form of care. If the system is attentive, then something good is assumed to be happening. But attention alone can be enough to diffuse pressure. It can reframe urgency into a "we are still talking" posture. The pace of talk becomes the pace of accountability. As long as conversation continues, closure is postponed.

The analytic tone of discussion is itself a kind of reward. It makes people feel intelligent, coherent, recognized. They hear their own words mirrored back by others. They feel the texture of agreement. The emotional satisfaction is real, and it can be mistaken for the progress of judgment.

Discussion also has a reputation of fairness. It appears to give everyone a chance. It appears to be non-coercive. But fairness in conversation is not the same as fairness in authority. A system can allow equal speech time while preserving unequal decision routes. The disguise works because the surface feels equitable, while the structure remains unchanged.

The medium of discussion has a subtle effect. It privileges clarity, coherence, and fluency. Those who can frame recognition in accepted language appear more influential. This is not necessarily manipulation. It is a property of the medium. When authority is absent, fluency becomes a substitute for power, and recognition begins to compete on rhetorical grounds rather than structural ones.

They offer feedback channels.

A feedback channel formalizes listening. It takes private recognition and makes it legible. It gives the impression of a pathway, as if the act of submission creates a trajectory. The channel looks like a route, and the mind often completes the route for it.

The channel can be designed with care. It can be anonymous. It can be welcoming. It can be celebrated by the system as a sign of openness. These details matter to the person who speaks, but they do not determine whether the system is obligated to change. The channel is a membrane, not a guarantee.

The existence of a channel suggests that someone will respond. Not necessarily immediately, not necessarily publicly, not necessarily with change, but the implication is there. That implication is enough to turn recognition into a subtle obligation: if the channel exists, then silence begins to feel like neglect. People send messages not because they expect authority, but because it is hard to sit with clear recognition without release.

A channel can be perfectly respectful and still be a disguise. Respectful listening is not the same as obligation to change. The difference is not visible in the interface. It lives in the unseen commitments of the system, in the way decisions actually move once the feedback is collected.

Channels also create a sense of record. Recognition becomes archived. It becomes a data point, a ticket, a line in a spreadsheet. That record can be soothing. It means the recognition is not lost. Yet records do not act. They wait. They depend on a separate mechanism of authority that may or may not exist.

The backlog of recognition can grow quietly. People can learn that their message has been received, that it is "in review," that it is "being considered." These phrases are not dishonest. They simply do not describe authority. They describe attention. The disguise relies on the overlap between attention and decision, knowing that attention is easier to offer.

They offer meetings, reviews, retrospectives, and postmortems.

These are ritual forms of recognition. They are moments when the system agrees to look at itself. A review acknowledges that judgment has already occurred elsewhere. A retrospective admits that outcomes have meanings. A postmortem signals that the system is willing to be honest.

These rituals can be necessary. They can be serious. They can be emotionally costly. But they are still not judgment. They are reflections on judgment. They take the shape of action without the risk of action. They can produce clarity without producing movement.

Rituals of reflection are powerful because they feel like accountability. People tell the truth. They admit error. They name patterns. The group witnesses. That witness can feel like a form of repair. It is not nothing. Yet if authority is not present, then the ritual does not bind the system to change. The ritual becomes a kind of honesty that is insulated from consequence.

Clarity without movement is often experienced as a kind of suspense. The mind expects alignment between what is seen and what is done. When the alignment is absent, people feel a low-level dissonance, a quiet impatience, a subtle embarrassment. The culture of action bias intensifies this. If clarity is public, inaction is treated as failure. So the system offers rituals of clarity, then quietly keeps its pathways intact.

Suspense can become a habit. People learn to live inside it. They anticipate change that does not arrive. They become skilled at articulating what is wrong, and less confident that the articulation matters. This creates a strange rhythm. Recognition spikes during the ritual, then collapses into normalcy afterward. The system appears to learn, while the structure stays the same.

These feel participatory. They feel meaningful. They feel close to judgment.

They are not judgment.

Participation is not the same as authority. Participation can exist within a bounded space where outcomes are already stabilized. Meaning can be present without leverage. The feeling of closeness can be accurate about atmosphere, while inaccurate about consequence. This is why the disguise can persist even among thoughtful people. It does not require naivete. It only requires the human tendency to equate being heard with being able to decide.

Participation can also be emotionally binding. When people contribute to a conversation, they become invested in the group. They carry a piece of the shared recognition. That investment can create a sense of ownership. Ownership is not authority. It is a feeling of responsibility that does not guarantee control. The disguise thrives on that overlap.

The closeness is also social. When people gather to discuss, the shared recognition creates a sense of collective presence. That presence can be mistaken for power. But power in this context is not a feeling. It is a route through which judgment travels and becomes binding. If the route is missing, the feeling stays, and the consequence does not.

The mismatch between presence and power can distort identity. People may come to define themselves by their participation, by their knowledge of the issues, by their role in the conversation. When authority is absent, those identities are fragile. They depend on a system that can value recognition without granting it consequence. This fragility is another quiet cost of the disguise.

The key difference is subtle but decisive.

In these spaces, nothing is required to change.

Obligation is the hinge. Judgment Authority does not just permit a decision; it carries a structural expectation that the decision can alter the system. Without that expectation, recognition floats. It can be intense, nuanced, clear, and still remain suspended.

The word "change" can hide several layers. Sometimes change means a public announcement. Sometimes it means a shift in policy. Sometimes it means a quiet reallocation of attention. In a system without authority, none of these are required, so the system can choose the least disruptive form of movement, or no movement at all, while still appearing responsive.

The difference can be invisible in the moment. The language of the meeting may sound like action. The tone may feel like commitment. But if the system is not bound to respond, then the recognition becomes a kind of ambient truth, known but not enacted.

Ambient truth can be strangely stable. It does not fade. It hovers. People return to it. They repeat it in new meetings, bring it into new documents, attach it to new events. The system accumulates clarity, while the path of authority remains fixed.

Transparency can make this feel acceptable. If the truth is visible, the system appears honest. Honesty is meaningful, but it is not the same as authority. A system can be transparent about its limits and still be structurally closed to change. The truth can be on the table, and the table can still be bolted down.

In some environments, clarity becomes a kind of prestige. Those who can articulate the situation well gain recognition for their insight. The recognition is deserved. Yet it can also become a substitute for change. The system rewards articulation because articulation does not threaten it. The disguise is sustained by celebrating clarity while keeping authority untouched.

Repeated acknowledgment can have a hypnotic effect. Each time the truth is restated, it feels closer to resolution. But repetition does not create obligation. It can even normalize the absence, turning the lack of authority into a familiar background fact. People adapt. They learn to live with the gap as if it were simply part of the environment.

The language of processöften appears here. Process suggests movement, care, and fairness. It can be all of those. But process without authority is still process. It can stabilize the system while leaving the decision routes unchanged. The disguise is that the process feels like progress, even when it is only motion.

In cultures that prize action, ambient truth can be uncomfortable. It implies that things can be understood and still remain unchanged. It implies that the value of recognition is not always instrumental. That runs against a common assumption that understanding is only worthwhile if it leads to visible movement. The disguise uses this assumption. It allows recognition to be celebrated while action remains optional.

The system may even introduce small motions that look like change but do not alter the core. A new committee may be formed. A new initiative may be named. A pilot may be announced. These gestures can be sincere, but they can also serve as confirmations of responsiveness without touching the central route of authority. Recognition is thus acknowledged, action is performed, and the deeper structure stays intact.

You may speak. You may explain. You may even convince.

But no obligation exists for the system to update itself based on what you say.

The words are not wasted. They can change how people see. They can shape internal narratives. They can influence future conversations. But they do not bind the system. The system can absorb them, express appreciation, and then continue along the same path.

The response can be warm. It can include gratitude, recognition of effort, and a sense that the issue is understood. These are real responses. They can relieve immediate tension. But they do not create obligation. The system can be grateful without being accountable. This is a subtle but important distinction.

The difference between influence and authority is not always visible. Influence can be sincere. It can be potent. It can also be reversible. Authority is not reversible in the same way. It is designed to withstand ambivalence. When authority is absent, influence is the strongest available currency, and the system can accept it without paying back in change.

This is a delicate kind of politeness. The system does not reject your recognition. It does not silence it. It invites it, then brackets it. The bracket is what turns recognition into a safe substance.

The bracket is an invisible boundary. Inside it, recognition can be celebrated. Outside it, the structure remains untouched. People often sense the boundary without being able to name it. They feel that some observations are "useful" while others are merely "noted." Both can be true. Only one carries authority.

Recognition inside the bracket can become a kind of currency. It is traded for goodwill, for reputation, for inclusion. This is not necessarily manipulation. It is the social economy that emerges when authority is scarce. The disguise persists because recognition still has value, even when it does not change outcomes.

This creates a dangerous illusion: the illusion of near-authority.

Close enough to feel responsible. Far enough to be powerless.

Near-authority is psychologically demanding. It activates the sense of accountability without providing the route to act. The person feels implicated, not because they truly control outcomes, but because they have been asked to see clearly. Seeing clearly can feel like a promise. The mind treats recognition as a bond. If the bond is never honored, people feel subtle guilt, or a sense that they have failed a responsibility that was never theirs.

Near-authority also produces a kind of reputational risk. If one speaks with precision, others assume one has leverage. When the system does not move, observers infer that the speaker chose not to act. The absence of authority is misread as a choice. This can create tension between people, not because anyone intends harm, but because the structure is hidden.

This is where action bias becomes cruel. It insists that recognition must lead to action, then places recognition in a space that cannot act. The individual carries the tension. The system remains unchanged. The disguise works by relocating pressure.

Near-authority also creates confusing signals about competence. If you can speak intelligently about a problem, it seems natural that you would be able to solve it. When the system does not allow that solution, people begin to question their own capability. They confuse structural limits with personal limits. The disguise turns structural absence into private doubt.

Private doubt can become internalized discipline. People reduce their recognition. They soften their language. They preempt their own clarity to avoid being blamed for inaction. Over time, this can make the system appear calmer, while the underlying absence persists. The disguise thus shapes not only structures, but the texture of speech and thought.

When speech softens, the system loses access to the sharpest signals of recognition. This is not because people have become less perceptive. It is because they have learned that clarity carries risk. The absence of authority is thus reinforced by a thinning of language. What is said becomes safer, less precise, more easily absorbed without consequence. The system sounds stable because the most destabilizing truths have been muted.

Another disguise is conditional authority.

You are told: "You can decide, if certain conditions are met."

The conditions are rarely explicit. They shift over time. They are evaluated by someone else.

Conditional authority mimics permission. It implies that a decision is possible, but only after a sequence of approvals, thresholds, or validation. Because the conditions are unclear, people try to infer them from small signals. They look for patterns, for tone, for unspoken rules. Recognition is redirected into decoding. This absorbs energy without yielding authority.

Conditional authority can be embedded in budgets, legal constraints, compliance requirements, or strategic priorities. Each of these can be real. Each can be necessary. But when they are opaque, they become a moving horizon. People are asked to aim, without being allowed to see the target. Recognition becomes a tool for navigation, not for decision.

Conditional authority also preserves plausible fairness. It suggests that the system is open, that anyone can decide if they meet the criteria. But if the criteria are held outside of view, then access to judgment becomes a moving target. The promise of authority exists without its reality.

The emotional effect is subtle. People continue to invest effort. They attempt to qualify themselves. They wait for the signal that the threshold has been crossed. In the meantime, they live in a state of suspended recognition, aware of what could be decided but unable to decide it.

Suspension produces its own culture. People trade stories about what the conditions might be. They interpret silence as feedback. They reframe setbacks as signs of being "not ready yet." The system does not need to enforce this. The absence of clarity invites it. Conditional authority thus creates an environment in which recognition is constantly re-aimed at the condition itself, not the decision.

As a result, effort accumulates without clarity about whether it will ever convert into authority.

People invest energy hoping to cross an invisible threshold.

Often, the threshold does not exist.

The accumulation of effort can look like progress. Projects move. Documents are refined. Arguments become sharper. But the central question remains untouched. If the system does not grant authority, then the movement becomes a loop. Recognition is circulated within the loop, never resolving into decision.

Loops can be productive in a technical sense. They create learning. They improve articulation. They refine plans. But without authority, they do not end. They can become self-sustaining, where the work of preparation becomes the work itself. The system appears energetic, while the actual decision remains deferred.

The invisible threshold is a powerful device. It keeps attention oriented toward the future, where authority is imagined to arrive. The future becomes a justification for present endurance. The disguise is not in the claim that authority is possible, but in the absence of proof that authority is ever granted.

In such environments, people can become experts at preparation. They can become eloquent about readiness. They can describe the conditions with great sophistication, without ever being able to show that the conditions lead anywhere. Recognition becomes a form of rehearsal, which can feel meaningful even when it never becomes performance.

Rehearsal has its own aesthetic. It carries the promise of a future event. It feels like progress even in the absence of a stage. The system can survive on rehearsal, provided the participants remain willing to invest. The disguise is that rehearsal feels like proximity to authority, when it is often only proximity to possibility.

There is also symbolic authority.

Titles, labels, and roles suggest judgment power, while the actual decision routes bypass them.

This mismatch is especially common in modern organizations.

Symbols matter because they provide orientation. A title is supposed to signal a zone of control. A role is supposed to indicate a boundary of responsibility. When the symbol does not match the route of authority, people operate under false maps. They assume that recognition can travel through the titled person, only to discover that the route leads around them.

Symbolic authority is not always cynical. It can emerge from the desire to honor expertise without redesigning structure. It can emerge from history, from legacy titles that no longer correspond to actual power. It can emerge from a need to communicate stability, even when authority is scattered elsewhere. The symbol serves the story. The route serves the decision. The gap between them is where disguise lives.

Symbols also serve external audiences. A title can reassure investors, partners, or the public. It signals that someone is "in charge," even if the actual decision path is distributed or hidden. This external function can pressure the system to maintain titles that no longer align with internal reality. The result is a widening gap between the narrative of authority and its actual movement.

The presence of symbolic authority changes the emotional climate. People may direct their recognition toward the symbol, believing that it will matter. When it does not, the recognition does not evaporate. It lingers. It is reinterpreted as failure, or as betrayal, or as evidence of hidden motives. The system does not need hidden motives to create this effect. It only needs a mismatch between symbol and route.

When recognition is repeatedly misdirected, trust becomes fragile. People begin to read signals more skeptically. They treat symbols as performative. This can erode cooperation, not because people are cynical, but because the map has failed them too many times. Symbolic authority thus risks undermining the very stability it was meant to communicate.

Symbolic authority absorbs blame efficiently.

When outcomes fail, the symbol is close enough to be held accountable, even if it was never close enough to decide.

This is one of the more painful disguises. It uses proximity to accountability to mimic authority. A person with a title is called to explain decisions they did not control. They are expected to answer for the system, because the symbol suggests ownership. The public memory attaches to them, not to the actual pathway. Recognition, again, is misdirected.

The efficiency of symbolic blame has a chilling effect. It teaches everyone else that proximity to recognition can be dangerous. It can reduce the willingness to speak, not because people are indifferent, but because speech seems to increase responsibility without increasing power. The system then becomes quieter, and the disguise becomes easier to maintain.

Blame also distorts the narrative of failure. If the symbol is held accountable, then the structural absence is obscured. Observers conclude that a person failed, not that the decision route was missing. This is convenient for the system. It preserves the illusion that authority exists, while punishing the person closest to the symbol.

Another disguise is moral framing.

Judgment is replaced by values.

Instead of asking: "What decision is structurally valid?" the system asks: "What would a good person choose?"

This shifts attention from authority to character.

People attempt to resolve structural gaps by improving themselves.

The gap remains.

Moral framing feels noble. It invites inner reflection. It turns conflict into a question of virtue. But virtue is not a route of authority. When the system uses moral framing, it moves recognition away from structure and into self-scrutiny. The individual becomes the site of resolution. The system stays intact.

Moral language can also be a form of social cohesion. It creates a shared vocabulary of good and bad. That shared vocabulary is powerful. It can align behavior, it can encourage care, it can reduce overt conflict. Yet when authority is missing, moral language can become a proxy for power. People debate values instead of confronting the fact that decisions are not available to them.

The moral question is often sincere. It can be asked in good faith. Yet the effect is to make recognition intensely personal. If you see a problem, then the burden of response is framed as a test of character. If no response is possible, then the person is left with a feeling of insufficiency. They know what is right. They cannot enact it. This produces a particular kind of quiet shame, which does not repair the structure, but does keep the person engaged.

The substitution of moral framing for authority also changes how disagreement is experienced. Disagreement becomes a sign of flawed character rather than a sign of a structural gap. People become cautious about acknowledging complexity. Recognition narrows. The system appears morally cohesive, while its authority remains undefined.

In this way, moral framing can be a highly effective disguise. It explains why recognition does not translate into action without admitting the absence of authority. It makes the lack of action appear as a lack of virtue, which can be corrected inside the person, not in the system.

Moral framing can also invite performative responses. People signal virtue to demonstrate that they care, not because it changes the structure. The system absorbs these signals, which reinforces the illusion that recognition has been addressed. The underlying route of authority remains hidden, while the moral atmosphere becomes more intense.

Urgency is another mask.

Crises compress time. Decisions appear to happen everywhere.

In reality, authority often centralizes further during urgency, while others experience increased pressure without increased control.

Urgency amplifies the culture of action bias. It insists that movement is the only form of responsibility. In that atmosphere, recognition that cannot become action feels intolerable. People push their observations into any available channel, hoping speed will convert attention into authority. The system absorbs the urgency, then reallocates authority to its narrowest core.

This creates a particular confusion. Because so much is happening, people assume that their recognition must matter. The noise of urgency sounds like access. But the sound is not the route. Decisions happen faster, not broader. The compression of time becomes a justification for exclusion. The disguise is that everyone feels involved, while fewer people can actually decide.

Urgency can also become habitual. A system can operate in a permanent state of crisis, where speed is normalized. In such contexts, recognition is always in motion, always urgent, always trying to attach itself to action. The constant pace can make it harder to see that authority has narrowed. The disguise thrives on exhaustion.

The discomfort of stillness becomes sharper during urgency. To remain still appears negligent. To acknowledge limits appears weak. Recognition without action feels like a moral failure. Yet the structural absence does not disappear. It is only hidden by speed.

The most effective disguise is hope.

Hope that effort will be recognized. Hope that clarity will emerge. Hope that someone is listening.

Hope delays exit.

Hope is a powerful stabilizer. It makes absence feel temporary. It transforms the lack of authority into a story of eventual arrival. That story can be enough to keep people engaged for long periods. They continue to offer recognition, not because they are naive, but because hope provides a bridge between what they see and what they believe might one day change.

Hope is also a social bond. When people share hope, they reinforce each other's willingness to stay. The atmosphere becomes one of mutual patience. The system can absorb that patience without changing its structure. The disguise works because hope feels generous. It feels constructive. It feels like a refusal of cynicism. But it can also serve as a substitute for authority.

There is a particular version of hope that is quiet and resilient. It does not demand immediate action. It simply assumes that recognition is building a record, that the record will be read, that the future will notice. This is a compelling story, especially in cultures that celebrate long-term perseverance. Yet the story does not itself create authority. It only makes the absence easier to tolerate.

Hope can be reinforced by small acknowledgments. A leader says they hear the concern. A report is commissioned. A plan is drafted. Each act can be interpreted as progress. Sometimes it is. Sometimes it is the maintenance of hope itself. Hope becomes self-sustaining, keeping recognition in place even when authority is absent.

Hope is ambiguous. It can be genuine care for the future, and it can be a way to survive the present. That ambiguity makes it resilient. People can hold hope and disappointment at the same time, because hope is not a claim about authority. It is a claim about possibility. Possibility can exist even when decision routes are closed.

The system benefits from this ambiguity. Hope stretches time. It allows recognition to remain active without insisting on immediate change. It creates a soft buffer between what is seen and what can be done. In that buffer, people continue to invest attention. The system gains stability, even if its authority has not expanded.

Hope also shapes memory. When people expect future change, they reinterpret the present as preparation. They see conversations as groundwork, and acknowledgments as signals, and delays as signs of carefulness. None of these interpretations are inherently false, but they can conceal the underlying absence. The story of future action can make the present feel purposeful even when authority is missing.

This is why hope is such a powerful disguise. It does not have to pretend that authority exists now. It only has to keep the idea of authority alive. Recognition remains engaged, not because it is misled, but because hope makes the gap bearable.

None of these disguises are necessarily malicious.

They often emerge naturally in systems trying to function without confronting uncomfortable asymmetries.

But their effect is consistent.

The absence of malice matters. It means the disguise can persist even among well-intentioned people. It means the system does not need conspirators. It only needs habits, rituals, and structures that prefer stability. These are common in any complex organization or community. They are not inherently bad. But they can create a persistent gap between recognition and authority.

The system may even experience itself as responsive. It listens. It convenes. It records. It reflects. These are genuine activities. They are not nothing. Yet they do not, by themselves, create obligation. The system can be active and still avoid change. The disguise is effective because it coexists with real work.

Activity can itself become a substitute for authority. People feel the motion of the system and assume that motion implies decision. But motion can be circular. It can be internal. It can be cosmetic. The system can stay in motion indefinitely while the route of judgment remains untouched. The disguise is not just in the lack of action, but in the presence of activity that is not binding.

In such environments, people often sense that something is missing, but they struggle to name it. The missing thing is not empathy, or intelligence, or effort. It is the structural link that makes recognition consequential. When the link is absent, recognition becomes a kind of parallel narrative, always adjacent to decision, rarely inside it.

Parallel narratives can feel rich. They can produce insight, new language, shared understanding. But they can also create a sense of unreality, as if the system is telling two stories at once: one about what is true, and another about what is done. The disguise survives because the stories coexist, allowing clarity to live alongside unchanged structure.

People remain engaged in places where their judgment does not land.

The engagement can be intense. It can be sincere. It can involve deep expertise. People may understand the problem in extraordinary detail. They may have nuanced interpretations, complex understandings of tradeoffs, and a clear sense of what is at stake. Recognition can be complete. The missing element is not clarity. It is binding consequence.

Binding consequence is the difference between recognition as understanding and recognition as decision. Without binding consequence, recognition is accurate but weightless. It can be shared, respected, remembered, and still remain outside the path of change. This is not a failure of recognition. It is a feature of authority.

This is where the chapter's decoupling becomes visible. Recognition does not obligate response. The system can acknowledge a truth and still be free to ignore it. The person can understand a situation and still be unable to change it. This decoupling is not a failure of recognition. It is a feature of the structure.

Cultural action bias makes this difficult to accept. It teaches that understanding is only valuable when it is instrumental. So when understanding does not move anything, people feel that they have failed to understand. They feel that their clarity is incomplete. But it is not incomplete. It is simply not empowered.

Action bias is reinforced by praise. People are admired for being decisive, for "doing something" in the face of ambiguity. The admiration creates pressure. It implies that recognition without movement is a kind of moral deficiency. In a system without authority, that pressure lands on individuals who cannot convert recognition into action. The disguise thus converts cultural ideals into private burdens.

This can produce a peculiar tension. One part of the mind insists that more recognition will solve the problem. Another part of the mind suspects that recognition is already sufficient. The system encourages the first part, because more recognition is harmless. It keeps people engaged. It keeps the appearance of responsiveness alive. It does not require authority.

The tension can endure for years. People cycle through renewed efforts to explain, to clarify, to present the issue differently. Each cycle is a form of hope. Each cycle is also a form of evidence that authority is still absent. Recognition becomes a repeated gesture, not because the recognition is wrong, but because the system does not move.

The discomfort of stillness appears again here. To recognize without moving feels like standing in front of an open door that cannot be used. The door is visible. The path is known. The inability to walk through it feels personal, even though it is structural. This is the emotional cost of the disguise. It converts structural absence into private unrest.

Unrest can take many forms. It can be restlessness, irritation, or a quiet numbness. It can be a sense of being stuck in analysis, a fear that one is overthinking, a suspicion that clarity itself is a problem. These feelings are not evidence of personal weakness. They are side effects of a structure that invites recognition without granting authority.

Recognizing disguise is not cynicism.

It is a form of orientation.

Once disguise is visible, the question changes from: "How do I make better judgments here?" to: "Is judgment expected of me at all?"

That question is quieter, but far more stabilizing.

The quietness matters. It does not demand immediate movement. It does not require a dramatic exit. It is simply a reorientation of perception, from the quality of judgment to the presence of authority. It allows recognition to settle into its proper place.

Orientation does not erase feeling. It does not remove the desire for change. It does not diminish the importance of what is recognized. It simply clarifies the contract of the system. When the contract is clear, recognition can exist without being pressed into action. The mind can stop interpreting every insight as a failed attempt at control.

When that orientation becomes possible, recognition can be held without coercion to act. The mind can acknowledge what is real without turning that acknowledgement into a demand. This does not solve the structural absence. It does not repair the system. But it clarifies what the system is and is not asking for. It replaces the illusion of near-authority with a more stable understanding of the actual arrangement.

Stability here does not mean comfort. It means a reduction in confusion. It means that the person no longer has to interpret recognition as a hidden obligation. Recognition can be complete without being compelled. Action may or may not follow, but recognition no longer carries the false promise that it must.

The decoupling can feel disappointing, because it removes the fantasy that recognition alone can move structures. At the same time, it can feel clarifying, because it removes the expectation that every insight is a form of responsibility. Recognition becomes what it is: an accurate understanding of the situation, not a mandate.

This is the decoupling at the center of the chapter. Recognition exists as a separate kind of truth, not as a prelude to action, not as a test of character, not as a demand for movement. The system's disguises become legible under this light. They remain what they are, but they lose their power to confuse.

The final shift is subtle. It is not a solution, and it is not a directive. It is a clearer description of the terrain. Where authority is absent, recognition is still possible, meaning is still possible, clarity is still possible. What is not guaranteed is that any of this will obligate response.

The chapter ends with that distinction, not as advice, but as a description of a common pattern. The pattern is the presence of recognition inside structures that do not require change. Once this is seen, the disguise is less convincing, and the absence is easier to name.

Chapter 9

Recognition without resolution

Recognition does not arrive as relief.

It arrives as quiet.

Quiet is the opposite of the story people expect. Relief has a shape that can be shared. It comes with a visible exhale, a moment that can be named. Quiet does not come with a name. It is not celebratory and not tragic. It does not ask for congratulations. It does not ask for pity. It is the absence of the pressure to perform a verdict. The lack of a verdict can feel like nothing has happened, which is exactly why others so often read it as failure. If there is no obvious win, if there is no visible movement, if there is no speech to match the moment, the social imagination collapses into the simplest explanation: stopping. And stopping is narratively coded as losing.

The expectation of relief is a social inheritance. Most people are trained to believe that recognition is the moment when a struggle ends and a choice begins. Recognition is imagined as a turning point, as if a door opens and the person steps through it. When recognition instead produces stillness, it violates the script. The audience waits for a sentence to end, and it does not end. The person waiting inside the quiet feels that gap as exposure, as if a spotlight has turned on without a stage direction. This is the beginning of exit stigma. The gap is read as a missing success, not as a realistic description of what was never possible.

An ending without a verdict feels like a broken promise. People are trained to see effort as a narrative with a climax. If no climax appears, the story is assumed to have failed. This is why stopping is not read as neutral. It is read as the missing final scene. The person is expected to deliver that scene. When they do not, others deliver it for them. The delivered scene is almost always the same, a person who could not finish, a person who lost resolve, a person who was not strong enough for the pressure. These variations are comforting because they are personal. They turn structural silence into a character trait. The quiet moment becomes evidence of weakness, rather than evidence of a closed system. So the quiet is not allowed to be quiet. It is translated into a story that can be told, and in that translation, the stopping is cast as failure.

When someone finally sees that judgment authority is absent, the first reaction is rarely action.

It is stillness.

Stillness is not the same as peace. It is the pause of a body that has been braced for a long time and is unsure how to exist without the brace. It is the moment after a loud room falls silent, when the ears are still ringing. In settings where constant motion is read as competence, stillness looks like withdrawal. In settings where momentum is read as virtue, stillness looks like defeat. The absence of visible motion is not neutral in a group. It asks others to tolerate a gap in the narrative, and most people do not. They fill it in. They name it. They label it. The label is usually failure.

Stillness threatens the shared story of progress. Stories are structured around action. Action implies agency. Agency implies that outcomes are earned. If action stops without a visible prize, then the story has to change. Instead of changing the story, observers often change the person. They reclassify the stillness as weakness, confusion, or loss of will. This is the narrative bias at work. It is not malicious. It is convenient. It protects the belief that the system still works and that the right kind of motion would still be rewarded.

In many settings, the bias is institutional. Progress is tracked, summarized, and displayed. Status becomes a performance in its own right. When a person has no update, the absence is treated as a warning signal. Stillness is reclassified as underperformance, not because anyone has proof, but because the metrics demand a result. The narrative of progress is embedded in the language of goals, milestones, and reports. If there is no milestone, then there is no progress. If there is no progress, then the person must be failing. This logic is simple, which makes it difficult to dislodge. It turns a pause in judgment into a visible defect on a dashboard, and the dashboard becomes the authority.

This stillness is often misinterpreted.

From the outside, it looks like disengagement. From the inside, it feels like suspension.

Suspension has its own gravity. It is not a declaration that nothing matters. It is the moment after a structure is revealed as closed, when the body is waiting for the weight of that fact to settle. The person in suspension is not refusing to try. They are refusing to pretend that trying is the same as influence. That refusal does not read well to observers, especially those invested in the old story. They prefer the clarity of a failure narrative to the ambiguity of a structural diagnosis. A failure narrative has a hero and a mistake. A structural diagnosis has no hero, only a map that never included authority.

Suspension is a social contradiction. It signals neither loyalty nor exit. Others do not know how to position themselves around it. Some try to pull the person back into motion. Others step away to avoid the uncertainty. The person can feel the subtle change in how they are treated, as if their value is being tested by speed. The test is not explicit, but it is felt in the patience that runs out, in the questions that repeat, in the assumption that a delay must indicate weakness. Stillness becomes a kind of exam, and the inability to offer a clear answer becomes evidence against the person. This is another way the failure narrative asserts itself.

Suspension also creates interpersonal discomfort. People who are still engaged in the struggle fear that suspension is contagious. They feel the possibility that their own momentum might be questioned. So they press for a reason, a plan, a new declaration. The pressure is not always hostile. It can be expressed as concern, as offers of help, as invitations to rejoin the race. But the subtext is often the same: stillness must be temporary, because a lasting pause would threaten the premise that the race is meaningful.

Suspension touches identity as well as momentum. If a person has been known as the one who persists, the pause is read as a break in character. Others begin to speak as if they are no longer the same person. Labels appear quickly, often in whispered forms of concern: burned out, disillusioned, lost. These labels compress a complex recognition into a simple decline narrative. They allow the group to keep its story and to place the disruption safely inside one individual. The person in suspension can feel this shift as a sudden collapse of social recognition, as if their identity depended on motion and has vanished with it.

Energy that was previously consumed by justification has nowhere to go.

There is no immediate replacement task.

Justification is exhausting because it pretends to be productive. It requires constant rehearsal. It demands explanations for why a closed structure will open any minute. When it disappears, there is a sudden quiet in the mind and in the calendar. Nothing rushes in to fill it, not because there is no work to do, but because the work that had been done was not actually work. It was performance of certainty. When the performance stops, the stage is still lit. That stillness is exposed. It feels like being seen without a script.

The emptiness that follows is not a new problem. It is the shape of the old problem, now visible without the costume. People around it are tempted to fill it with tasks because tasks are legible. They want to know what is being done, what is being built, what can be measured. A pause that cannot be measured is treated as a lack of commitment. The person in the pause is interpreted as someone who has dropped the ball. Yet the ball itself was a performance, rolling across a stage that never connected to an actual game.

Time opens up in a way that can feel unreal. Hours that were once filled with explanations now stretch without purpose. The mind circles the same moments, not to solve them, but because they are the last points where the old story still felt true. This is not planning. It is a reprocessing of the scene without the familiar scripts. To outsiders, this looks like hesitation. To the person inside it, it feels like the slow settling of a truth that cannot be argued away.

Restlessness can appear in this open time. It is not a signal to act, but a sign of how accustomed the body is to urgency. The person may feel pressure to explain the restlessness, to present it as intention, to find a story that justifies the pause. The effort to narrate the pause reactivates the old justification loop. That loop is familiar, so it feels safe, but it is also the engine that produced the misalignment. The cycle between restlessness and explanation is another subtle way the failure narrative is generated, because it treats quiet as a deficiency that must be fixed.

Many people try to rush through this phase.

They look for a new framework. A new role. A new place where judgment might land.

The rush is not only personal. It is social. People around them want a resolution they can understand. They want a replacement narrative to stabilize their own sense of order. So the search for a new place is encouraged, celebrated, sometimes demanded. The moment of suspension is treated as a malfunction instead of a necessary pause in perception. That pressure turns recognition into a kind of embarrassment: if there is no next move, then the recognition itself is judged as a failure to act.

Busyness carries social capital. People are praised for being needed, for having more to do than time allows, for staying inside the current of activity. To stop is to risk losing that capital. It is not only the loss of tasks, but the loss of a visible signal of worth. This is why the urge to reattach can be so intense. The person is not only seeking a new role; they are seeking the return of a status that was tied to visible motion. The culture treats that motion as evidence of value, and without it, the person feels exposed to misreading.

The desire for a new framework often masks a deeper fear. A framework provides a promise: if the right rules can be found, then authority will reappear, and the story will resume. The absence of authority feels like a void, and many people are trained to fill voids with systems, with roles, with fresh duties. The urgency to refill the space does not mean the recognition was shallow. It means the social world is built to reward visible activity, not accurate stillness.

But recognition does not demand movement.

It demands accuracy.

Accuracy is not a virtue in the way the culture uses the word. It is not a badge. It is a description of the system that no longer lies. Recognition insists that what was structurally closed be called closed. It refuses to pretend that a door is open just because effort is visible. That refusal is, in itself, a kind of stopping, which is why it is so often called failure by those who need the door open.

Accuracy can be lonely. It strips away the social comfort that comes from mutual illusion. When a group pretends a door is open, there is a sense of shared purpose. Accuracy breaks that consensus. It does not ask anyone to agree. It simply names the boundary. The person who names the boundary is rarely thanked. They are more often seen as the reason the story cannot continue. This is another way that stopping becomes stigmatized.

Accuracy can feel like a social risk. Naming a boundary can be interpreted as disloyalty. Pointing to closure can be heard as sabotage. Those who are still invested may distance themselves from the person who names it, not because they disagree, but because acknowledging the boundary would implicate their own efforts. So the act of accurate recognition creates a subtle exile. The person becomes the one who sees too much and asks for too little, and that position is rarely celebrated. It is easier to treat them as pessimistic than to face the cost of accepting their clarity.

Optimism is often treated as loyalty. In environments that depend on hope, naming a boundary is interpreted as negativity. The person who speaks accurately is asked to be more positive, which is another way of asking them to rejoin the illusion. When they do not, they are seen as dragging the group down. This social pressure does not argue against the recognition. It simply reclassifies it as attitude. The recognition is reduced to mood, and the person is reduced to the mood. That reduction erases the structural insight and turns it into a personality flaw, another path by which stopping is coded as failure.

Accuracy about what has already happened.

About how much effort was spent attempting to resolve something that was never structurally open.

What has already happened is not just a sequence of events. It is also a record of misread signals, of promises that never carried authority, of tasks that looked like progress but were only movement. In hindsight, those movements are judged as waste, not because they were foolish, but because they were directed at a target that could not receive them. Retrospective judgment is blunt. It does not see the uncertainty of the past. It sees a clean line from effort to non-outcome and calls the effort a mistake. That is the narrative bias. The story wants an ending, and so it edits the middle.

Hindsight cleans the timeline. The messy middle is removed, and the remaining arc looks inevitable. Continuing is romanticized as courage. Stopping is recast as a flaw. The person who stopped is framed as the one who could not take the pressure, and that framing becomes a lesson others can hold onto without changing their assumptions. This is retrospective judgment as a social force. It reshapes memory, and it reshapes identity, until the stop itself feels like the only thing others remember.

Retrospective judgment is also social. A group rewrites the past to keep its own identity intact. If the group believes its goals were always clear, then the person who stopped must have lacked dedication. If the group believes its leaders were always wise, then the person who stopped must have lacked discipline. The narrative is rearranged so that the structure remains legitimate. The cost of that rearrangement is the person's credibility. They are remembered as the one who quit, not the one who noticed the absence of authority.

Once the story has been rewritten, the rewrite becomes evidence. People speak of signs they claim they noticed earlier. They insist the outcome was obvious. This retroactive certainty erases the uncertainty of the moment and casts the stop as a lack of courage. The person becomes a cautionary tale, not because their actions were uniquely flawed, but because the group needs a lesson that does not require revising the structure. The stop is framed as a warning, and the warning is used to reinforce the demand to keep going.

This is why stopping is so easy to misread. It looks like a personal choice because that is the only frame the story can tolerate. Structural closure is not a satisfying ending. It does not fit the arc of effort and reward. So the story becomes about a person who failed to keep going, or who could not handle the pressure, or who lost the will to fight. Each of these interpretations has the advantage of simplicity. Each of them preserves the myth that persistence would have been rewarded.

This accounting is uncomfortable.

Not because of failure, but because of misalignment.

Misalignment is less dramatic than failure and more corrosive. Failure implies a clear attempt and a clear result. Misalignment implies a prolonged state of aiming at a place that could not register the aim. There is grief in that realization, but it is not the grief of defeat. It is the grief of time spent in a role that was never positioned to matter in the way it promised. That grief often gets translated into shame, not because shame fits, but because shame is a socially legible emotion.

Identity built on endurance has few places to go when endurance no longer feels meaningful. The self had been measured by the capacity to continue, and now continuation looks like a performance without consequence. This creates a hollowing effect. The person can feel as if the center of their identity has been removed, leaving behind a shell that still moves but no longer knows why. Others may continue to praise resilience, not realizing that the praise now falls on an empty category. The praise itself can sound like an accusation, as if the person has failed to live up to the very identity they are being asked to maintain.

Misalignment also erodes trust in one's own perceptions. If the signals were misleading, then the mind begins to doubt its ability to read signals at all. This is the quieter part of identity collapse. The person wonders whether their instincts are permanently compromised. The question is not announced. It is felt. It sits behind every new invitation, behind every new promise, like a shadow that cannot be shaken. This is not a lesson. It is a residue.

You realize that you were not wrong. You were simply positioned elsewhere than you believed.

Position is not only literal. It is the way a system assigns leverage, the way a group grants or withholds impact. Being positioned elsewhere means the signals you read were not made for you, the commitments you assumed were not binding, the promises you tried to honor were not authorized. It is possible to have acted with full sincerity inside a map that did not include you as an agent. That is not an error of character. It is an error of map.

This difference is hard to convey because most social narratives collapse it. They treat location as a function of effort, as if someone can move into authority simply by trying hard enough. But authority is a position granted, not a position achieved. When it is absent, trying harder does not create it. Realizing this is not the same as blaming the system. It is the clear recognition that the system was not built to respond. Stopping is the visible consequence of that invisible fact.

At this stage, there is a strong temptation to turn recognition into morality.

To ask: "Was I naive?" "Should I have known better?" "Was this my responsibility?"

The moral turn is seductive because it restores the sense that someone must be accountable. If there is no authority and no clean outcome, moralizing the situation creates a judge and a sentence. The judge is the self. The sentence is a story of personal inadequacy. That story is socially satisfying. It allows observers to keep their faith in the structure. If the person failed because of a flaw, then the system remains intact. The cost of that story is the collapse of identity for the one who accepts it. Identity was built on effort, effort now appears as mistake, so the self becomes suspect. This is how stopping looks like failure from the inside.

The moral narrative also protects others from discomfort. If one person is flawed, then others do not need to question their own positions. They can keep moving, confident that the right kind of character will be rewarded. This is why moral judgment gathers speed. It is easy to circulate. It offers closure. It can be expressed in a sentence. It is much harder to sit with the possibility that a structure itself cannot deliver what it promises. That possibility is destabilizing. So the moral story wins.

For the person inside the story, this moral frame can become a compulsion. They may try to compensate, to prove that the stop was not weakness, to show that they are still capable. The impulse does not resolve the recognition. It only adds new performances on top of it. Others may interpret this renewed effort as a return to the right path, which reinforces the moral frame. The person then feels the pressure to sustain the performance, even though it no longer feels honest. Shame becomes productive, which is another way the system keeps moving.

These questions reintroduce judgment where judgment is no longer relevant.
They attempt to restore meaning through self-assessment.

Self-assessment can be a mirror or a trap. In this context it becomes a trap because it asks personal questions about a structural condition. The individual becomes the site of explanation for a system that refused to authorize judgment in the first place. That misplacement creates a second harm. The first harm was wasted effort. The second is the distortion of self-understanding.

Distortion shows up as a narrowing of the self. The person begins to define themselves by the moment they stopped. Everything before is reevaluated through that lens. Every choice becomes suspect. The language of personal failure overwrites the language of structural reality. The person is left with a story in which they are the problem, which is a story that feels actionable but is not accurate.

Once the self is narrowed, language follows. The person begins to describe themselves as someone who failed. The description becomes a social cue, and others treat them accordingly. The narrative loops. Being treated as failure confirms the internal story, which makes it harder to hold the structural recognition in view. This is how identity collapse becomes durable, not because the recognition was wrong, but because the surrounding mirrors only show one image.

But recognition is not a verdict on character.

It is a correction of location.

A correction of location does not resolve everything. It does not undo the time spent. It does not grant new authority. It only changes the axis of interpretation. It says: the problem was not hidden in the self. The problem was the assumption that the self had standing within a closed structure. That is a different kind of sentence. It is not flattering, not condemning. It is simply accurate.

The difficulty is that accuracy sounds cold. It lacks the warmth of moral stories. It lacks the excitement of a redemption arc. A correction of location does not offer an identity to replace the old one. It only creates space where identity can no longer rest on the illusion of influence. That space feels empty. It invites interpretation. Others fill it with their own projections. The person inside it feels both relief and loss without an audience willing to accept that complexity.

Another temptation is to convert recognition into advice.

To warn others. To explain the structure. To help them avoid the same trap.

Advice allows recognition to be displayed. It becomes a public artifact: proof that something was learned, proof that the time was not wasted. It also offers a way to regain a sense of authority by becoming the person who sees what others do not. Yet advice rarely lands with the weight intended. The person receiving it does not share the same history of cost, so the warning can sound abstract, or worse, self-righteous. In that moment, recognition is misread again, this time as a claim to superiority.

Advice can also be heard as accusation. If someone is still investing effort in a structure that feels meaningful to them, hearing that the structure is closed can sound like an attack on their choices. The advice is then rejected not because it is false, but because accepting it would require a painful reorientation. So the speaker is dismissed as bitter, or as someone who lacks persistence. The recognition returns to isolation, framed again as failure.

This creates a double bind around speech. If the person explains themselves, the explanation is heard as excuse. If they remain silent, the silence is heard as guilt. Either way, the public narrative is not corrected. The space for nuanced recognition narrows, and the simplest interpretation wins. That is why quiet persists. It is not always chosen. It is often the least distortive option in a world that rewards simple endings.

Sometimes this helps. Often it does not.

Helpfulness is not a property of the message alone. It is a property of timing, of readiness, of the listener's need to preserve their own narrative. If they are still inside the structure, they may need the hope that it is open. To hear that it is closed is to hear that their effort has no home. That is a violent idea to accept without personal evidence. So the advice passes by, and the recognizer is left with the quiet again, now tinged with the sense of being unable to translate it.

This is a cruel paradox. The person who sees the absence of authority cannot deliver that sight to others. The person who has not yet paid the cost cannot fully register the warning. Between them is a gap in understanding that feels like a personal failure, when it is actually a difference in position. The gap becomes another reason for the world to conclude that stopping is a weakness, not a recognition.

Recognition that cannot be shared easily becomes private knowledge. Private knowledge has little social power. It cannot defend itself in meetings or in memory. Over time, the person watches their understanding shrink in the public story. The story becomes simplified. It becomes easier for others to say that stopping was just giving up. The person knows this is not true, but without a shared language, the knowledge stays internal. This is the quiet cost of recognition: it is accurate, but it cannot win in a public narrative.

People cannot see absence of authority until they encounter its cost personally.

Explanation does not substitute experience.

Experience is not a requirement that can be imposed. It is not something one person can deliver to another. When the cost arrives, it rearranges the map of the world in ways that talk cannot. This is why stopping is so often misread as failure by those who have not yet encountered the cost. They are still inside the story that effort and outcome are linked. The person who has stepped outside that story appears to them as someone who simply quit. The gap between these perceptions is wide and not easily bridged.

When recognition surfaces, it can look impulsive from the outside. Observers see a single decision where the person felt a long accumulation. They assume the stop was sudden because they did not feel the slow pressure. This misunderstanding intensifies the stigma. An action that is finally named after months or years of friction is treated as a dramatic retreat, and the narrative of failure grows stronger precisely because the history was invisible.

The cost is not always dramatic. Sometimes it is quiet and repetitive. It is the slow erosion of confidence, the ongoing friction between promise and reality, the accumulation of small evidences that the door is closed. When recognition finally happens, it is not a single event. It is a weight that has been gathering until the body can no longer ignore it. To observers, this looks like a sudden stop. To the person, it feels like a long delayed acknowledgement.

Recognition without resolution feels unfinished.

There is no ceremony. No external confirmation. No visible change.

Unfinishedness carries its own tension. The mind is trained to look for closure, so an open loop feels like a mistake. Others interpret the open loop as irresponsibility or avoidance. They wait for a statement that ends the chapter, and when it never arrives, they conclude that the person is stuck. The person is not stuck in a plan. They are living inside a reality that has no clean ending. That reality is hard to communicate, which leaves the unfinishedness intact and the failure narrative available.

A ceremony would give permission for others to accept the change. Without it, people search for familiar cues. They look for a new job title, a new project, a new enemy, a new victory. In the absence of those cues, recognition looks like collapse. This is how exit stigma is formed. The person is presumed to have failed because there is no proof of success. The recognition itself is not visible, so the only visible event is the stop.

Rituals are designed to stabilize meaning. They mark transitions, signal what has ended, announce what is allowed to begin. When recognition produces no ritual, the transition becomes socially illegible. Friends and colleagues ask for updates, not out of cruelty, but to place the person back into a story. The inability to provide that story is interpreted as a lack of progress, which is another way to call it failure. The person is left with a quiet that has no shared language.

Exit stigma does not end at the moment of stopping. It continues in the way credit is remembered, in the way contributions are retold, in the way the person is invited or not invited into future efforts. The story of failure becomes a lens through which their past is reinterpreted. What once looked like commitment is reframed as stubbornness. What once looked like leadership is reframed as overreach. The person's history is rewritten to justify the present narrative, and the rewrite makes the stigma durable.

And yet, something irreversible has occurred.

Irreversible does not mean triumphant. It means the old story can no longer be believed without conscious distortion. The person who has seen the absence of authority cannot unsee it, not because they are wiser, but because the pattern has been seen as a pattern. This knowledge is not empowering in the usual sense. It does not grant ability to change outcomes. It changes what outcomes are understood to be.

Irreversible also means a new kind of vulnerability. Once the old story is gone, there is no familiar script for what happens next. The person cannot easily reenter the performance without feeling the falseness of it. They may still participate, but the participation is transparent now, as if the stage lights have been turned up. The transparency is uncomfortable. It can look like cynicism from the outside, when it is more often a form of clarity that has nowhere to land.

Clarity without a home is easily misnamed. It is called cynicism because cynicism is a known category. Clarity is harder to classify. It does not denounce everything. It simply refuses to pretend. That refusal can feel like a threat to people who still need the performance. So the person who has recognized the absence is treated as disenchanted, as if disillusionment were a flaw, and that treatment adds another layer to the perception of failure.

With the old story gone, enthusiasm can feel performative. The person may still engage, but their energy has a different texture. Others notice the change and name it as lack of commitment. Invitations become cautious. Trust is withheld. The person is treated as someone who might stop again, which confirms the stigma. This is not punishment; it is a precaution built into the social world. But it amplifies the perception of failure, because the original stop continues to shape how future actions are interpreted.

You no longer mistake effort for influence.

You no longer confuse proximity with authority.

This change is often invisible to others. It does not announce itself. It is not a posture. It is a quiet recalibration of meaning. Effort can still be respected without being misread as power. Proximity can still be enjoyed without being mistaken for access. These are not strategies. They are shifts in perception that can neither be advertised nor made legible on demand.

An invisible shift creates a split between outward behavior and inward meaning. Roles may stay the same, conversations may continue, but the person no longer believes in the implied authority of the role. They may still participate, but with a different inner posture. This can feel like duplicity even when nothing is hidden. The self becomes layered: the public self continuing, the private self recognizing closure. This layer difference is another source of quiet, because speaking it feels like accusation in a world that depends on the performance. The person becomes harder to read, and that ambiguity invites others to impose their own narrative.

The shift is subtle. It does not eliminate the desire to try. It does not erase ambition. It simply removes the assumption that trying creates authority. That removal changes the emotional texture of effort. Work can still be done, relationships can still be maintained, plans can still be made, but the expectation attached to them is different. This difference is hard to explain without sounding detached. So it is often left unspoken, which keeps the misreading alive.

Ambiguity is often judged rather than understood. People prefer clear signals, and they interpret reservedness as indecision. The person feels the pressure to perform confidence in a system they no longer trust. The performance can resume temporarily, but it carries a sense of falsehood. The falsehood is not a lie. It is participation in a script that no longer convinces. This tension shows up in small moments: a pause before agreeing, a delay in enthusiasm, a softened refusal to argue. Those moments are read as weakness. The person experiences them as honesty. The gap widens.

This does not make you superior.

It makes you quieter.

Quiet here is not the silence of defeat. It is the silence of not needing to persuade. It is the absence of the ritual speech that typically follows a perceived win or loss. Without that speech, others are unsettled. They will narrate in your place, often choosing the simplest available narrative: that you failed, that you gave up, that you were not strong enough. The quiet does not correct them. It only continues to exist.

Quiet is rarely granted the dignity of complexity. In groups, silence is treated as assent or as sulking. In families, it is treated as distance or blame. The person who stops becomes the one who does not explain. The lack of explanation becomes an offense. Others feel deprived of their role in the story, so they push for a confession, a summary, a lesson. The person has none that fits. The truth is too structural, too abstract, too unsatisfying. So the quiet remains, and it is read as stubbornness. That reading intensifies the failure narrative.

Quiet also contains a kind of protection. Speech would invite debate, would invite others to reassert their stories. Silence prevents that, but it comes at a cost. The cost is misunderstanding. The person becomes a blank screen onto which others project their beliefs about grit, about loyalty, about success. In a world that values noise, that blankness looks like absence. Absence is often treated as failure.

Quiet is often mistaken for resignation.

In reality, it is calibration.

Calibration is not decisive action. It is the attempt to align perception with what has already been revealed. This alignment is slow because it is not merely intellectual. It is bodily. The body that once reacted to urgency now has to learn a different tempo. This looks like passivity from the outside. From the inside it looks like the work of untangling meaning from motion. That work has no visible milestone, which is why it is so often written off.

Calibration collides with external clocks. Deadlines still exist. Expectations still come. The person in calibration is not outside time; they are simply out of sync with the usual tempos. This mismatch creates friction. Others experience the pause as delay. They interpret it as indecision. The person experiences it as the time it takes for meaning to realign with reality. Because this process is internal, it is easy to dismiss. The dismissal makes the person feel isolated. The pause begins to feel like a private burden, which further reduces the desire to speak.

Calibration is also relational. It changes how a person hears promises, how they interpret invitations, how they assess loyalty.

The old reflexes are not immediately gone. They return in moments of pressure. The person becomes aware of how easily narratives can be reactivated, how quickly the urge to justify can return. The absence of a public script means this awareness remains private. It is another reason why the pause looks like failure to those outside it.

Before any decision can be made, the system must first be seen as it is.

Recognition completes that task, even when nothing else happens.

The phrase "nothing else happens" contains the whole problem. In a culture that equates meaning with movement, stillness is read as emptiness. But stillness is sometimes the only honest response to a structure that has been revealed as closed. The system is still there. The person is still there. The relationship between them has changed. That change cannot always be converted into action. It can only be held.

Recognition also changes the texture of decision. Decisions are no longer imagined as levers of control. They are seen as selections among limited consequences. This is not a technique. It is a sober view of how much influence remains. When asked for next steps, the person hesitates, not because they lack a plan, but because plans no longer promise authority. That hesitation is often read as drift. It is, instead, the visible edge of recognition: the refusal to pretend a lever exists where it does not.

Holding is not a resolution. It does not feel like progress. It does not provide a story for others to follow. Yet it is the only truthful stance when the system cannot be changed and the person cannot unsee what has been seen. This is why the moment can feel so lonely. The person is left with a truth that has no social ceremony, no professional marker, no obvious way to be recognized as real. The isolation is part of the cost.

The absence of resolution is not temporary in a predictable way. It can stretch without conclusion, which makes it hard for others to categorize. They may try to force a timeline onto it, asking when the pause will end, as if time itself could authorize closure. The person can feel that pressure as a demand for a verdict. Yet recognition is not a verdict. It is a description. Descriptions do not end the story. They only change the map. This difference is subtle to explain and easy to ignore, so the pressure persists.

Resolution may or may not follow.

Recognition stands on its own.

That standalone quality is part of the difficulty. Without a resolution, recognition cannot be exchanged for proof. It has no external artifact, no certificate, no outcome to point to. It exists as a shift in understanding, real to the person and invisible to everyone else. The invisibility keeps the failure narrative alive.

Standing on its own does not mean standing proudly. It means standing without the support of a narrative that other people recognize. It means living without the reassurance that an exit will be celebrated, or that a pause will be interpreted as wisdom. Stopping looks like failure because the culture is trained to see only one kind of ending. Recognition refuses that ending without offering a replacement. The refusal is quiet. The quiet remains.

Ongoing ambiguity becomes a quiet filter on relationships. Some people drift away because they cannot place the person in a familiar narrative. Others stay but reinterpret every pause as evidence that the person is unstable. The person experiences these shifts as a kind of social tax on accuracy. The tax is not announced, but it is paid in fewer invitations, smaller roles, guarded trust. This reinforces the sense that stopping has consequences beyond the moment itself. The recognition did not create those consequences, but it made them visible. In that visibility, the person sees how much of social belonging depends on performing the story of continuous motion.

Living with recognition means accepting that some stories will never resolve. The social world keeps asking for closure, and the person keeps living without it. The result is a long stretch of ambiguity that does not fit into calendars or milestones. It cannot be celebrated, and it is difficult to mourn. It is simply the ongoing fact of knowing where authority ends. That knowledge does not conclude the chapter. It leaves it open, which is why the stopping continues to look like failure to those who are still reading for an ending.

What remains is not a plan, and not a promise. It is a clearer map of where authority is absent and where effort will not be received. That clarity can be lived with, though it is not rewarded. It can be misunderstood, though it is accurate. Recognition does not resolve these tensions. It only makes them visible.

Chapter 10

Why action does not follow

After recognition, the most common question is still simple.

"What should I do now?"

The question feels natural. It feels responsible. It feels mature. It is also a question formed inside a culture that treats motion as virtue.

Action is taken as proof of care and membership. To act is to show that the situation matters, that other people matter, that a shared reality exists. To pause is to seem indifferent, even when the pause is not about indifference at all.

That culture does not pause when recognition arrives. It continues to assign meaning to presence and absence, continuation and withdrawal. Recognition changes perception, not conditions. Conditions are social.

The absence of judgment authority does not automatically create a new action space. It does not give a person permission that others can read. It does not carve out a stable social role for the one who has stopped compensating for what is missing.

In the private mind, recognition feels like clarity. In the social world, clarity is not a visible event. Other people cannot see it. They see only a shift in the pattern of participation.

Many readers expect this chapter to contain guidance. Steps. Principles. A way forward.

That expectation itself reveals how deeply action is associated with value. Insight is supposed to move. Silence is supposed to break. Continuity is supposed to hold.

But there are recognitions that do not point forward. They point sideways. They point inward. They stop pointing. The person who follows them does not become inactive. The person becomes careful about what can legitimately be done.

This chapter is not about how to move. It is about what is lost when one does not. Withdrawal carries real social penalties. They are not theoretical. They are not moralized advice. They are structural consequences of how people read each other.

Not continuing is not neutral. It is visible. It is interpreted. It can be experienced as a rupture even when it is an act of restraint. What looks like paralysis is often boundary recognition.

Not continuing does more than pause an action. It interrupts a rhythm that others have oriented themselves around. Social life is patterned. People make sense of each other by noticing what repeats. When repetition stops, the pattern breaks, and the break is experienced as a signal in its own right.

Continuation is often treated as proof of care. It is also treated as proof of belief. A person who keeps engaging is assumed to still endorse what the engagement implies. A person who stops engaging is assumed to have withdrawn that endorsement.

Because recognition is internal, others can only infer. Inference leans on familiar categories. People slot the withdrawal into explanations they already know, not into the subtlety of a boundary they cannot see.

Not continuing can be read as opting out of the group. It can be read as disloyalty, or as fragility, or as a signal of disinterest. These readings are not fair, but they are predictable. They are how groups protect coherence.

The person who withdraws may feel that they have stopped claiming authority. Others feel that they have stopped carrying their share. This asymmetry is not about intent. It is about the mismatch between private clarity and public coordination.

Social belonging depends on shared continuation. To stay inside a story, one must keep contributing to its momentum. When someone stops, they do not simply step aside. They are repositioned as a spectator in a story that continues without them.

Reciprocity sits underneath many expectations. People exchange judgments, interpretations, and the labor of making sense. Withdrawal interrupts the exchange. Others register the imbalance even if they do not name it.

There is rarely a ritual for this kind of withdrawal. Without a clear ending, others feel suspended. Suspension produces discomfort, and discomfort becomes narrative. The narrative becomes cost.

Not continuing can look like a refusal to join in collective risk. It can be read as a strategy for self protection. Even when it is a matter of intellectual honesty, it is interpreted in social terms.

These costs are the ground on which silence, drift, and recalibration occur. They are the ambient pressure that makes withdrawal feel heavier than it looks.

Silence is one of those costs. Silence looks neutral from inside. From the outside, it rarely is.

When someone stops arguing, stops pushing, stops volunteering meaning, a gap opens. The gap is filled. It is filled with assumptions, with rumors, with projections, with fear, with convenience.

Silence is read as refusal, read as agreement, read as contempt, read as exhaustion, read as calculation, read as cowardice. It can be read as all of these by different people at once.

The person who is silent may be trying to avoid the pretense of authority. But the audience does not know that. The audience only knows that something has stopped, that a familiar signal has gone quiet.

Silence becomes a medium because the social world cannot afford empty space. Groups require interpretation to coordinate. When interpretation is withheld, others interpret the withholding.

In a meeting, when a competent person ceases to offer judgment, the group does not hear an ethical boundary. It hears a lapse. The silence becomes a question and then a story.

That story may be practical. Perhaps the person is busy, perhaps distracted, perhaps less informed. But it can also become moral. The silence is read as a refusal to help, or a retreat from responsibility.

In a family, when someone stops containing conflict, stops translating tensions, stops smoothing edges, others experience the space as abandonment or protest. The absence becomes a kind of signal, regardless of intention.

In friendships, when someone stops initiating, stops explaining, stops clarifying, the absence becomes a quiet rebuke. Whether or not it is meant that way, it functions that way in the social imagination.

Silence is costly because it is not inert. It is a kind of speech that can never be fully controlled. The person who is silent cannot shape the meaning being assigned to the silence.

It is also costly because silence changes workload. Someone else must interpret. Someone else must decide. The quiet person may not be trying to shift the burden, but the burden shifts anyway.

This shift creates a social ledger. People feel the extra weight. They may not name it, but they register it. Silence becomes associated with the feeling of having to carry more alone.

Silence also has duration. A short pause is often read as deliberation. A long pause becomes absence. Absence becomes a new fact that others organize around. The cost grows as the pause stretches into a pattern.

Some roles are expected to speak. A supervisor is expected to clarify. A caregiver is expected to soothe. A mediator is expected to translate. Silence in these roles feels like abdication, regardless of the reason.

Silence can be read as passive aggression. People defend themselves against what they perceive as a quiet punishment. They become cautious. They share less. They preemptively retreat.

Without verbal repair, tension hardens. Small misunderstandings become fixed impressions. People stop giving the benefit of the doubt. Silence is not the only cause, but it is often the medium through which the hardening happens.

Silence can be contagious. Others reduce their own disclosure because they feel the channel is no longer safe or responsive. The collective tone shifts. Communication narrows. The gap widens.

When silence is broken, it can be treated as too late. Others have already updated. They have built routines that do not include the silent person. Reentry does not erase the time without response.

Silence often prompts tests. Others probe to see if the person still cares, still participates, still belongs. The probing feels like pressure, not like care. The silence grows heavier.

Silence is interpreted through past patterns. A person who was expressive is penalized more for quiet. A person who was always quiet is simply overlooked. The same behavior carries different weights.

Silence while physically present has its own weight. A person sits in the room, hears the conversation, but does not join. Others may experience this as being observed rather than joined. Observation without participation can feel like evaluation.

That feeling changes behavior. People edit themselves. They become cautious. They may avoid topics that they would have explored with a more engaged participant. The silence thus narrows what can be safely said.

This narrowing reduces intimacy. It makes the relationship less porous. Over time, people stop turning toward someone who is present but quiet, not out of punishment, but out of self protection.

In environments with strong norms, silence can look like disloyalty. The group expects visible support. Not speaking is taken as withholding solidarity. The person may still care, but the care is not audible, so it is treated as absent.

This produces a hard choice between honesty and belonging. The recognition that authority is absent can make speech feel false. The refusal to speak makes belonging feel fragile. The cost is the friction between these two truths.

Silence also removes small social comforts. The joke that used to soften tension, the quick word that used to repair a misunderstanding, are not offered. Without these micro repairs, relationships become brittle. Small tensions linger.

Brittleness changes the tone. People anticipate awkwardness. They approach with caution. Caution makes interaction thinner, and thin interaction reduces trust. The person who is silent is then met with even more caution.

Ambiguity is uncomfortable. When silence creates ambiguity, people resolve it by choosing a meaning that lets them move forward. That chosen meaning becomes a label. Labels are sticky.

The cost is not only what others think. It is how the silent person is met thereafter. Silence becomes the frame. The frame becomes the relationship.

In environments where speed matters, nonresponse is often treated as a form of dissent. It slows the group. It produces uncertainty. The group treats it as a problem to solve, not as a boundary to respect.

In slower environments, nonresponse can be more ambiguous, more prone to storytelling. People search for an explanation because the pace allows for rumination. Rumination becomes narrative.

Silence is also interpreted through the lens of status. When a high status person falls silent, others assume intent. When a low status person falls silent, others assume irrelevance. Both are penalties, just of different kinds.

The same silence can be seen as a strategic pause, as a thoughtful withdrawal, or as a lack of courage, depending on who holds it. The cost is not fixed. It is distributed by power.

Digital contexts intensify the visibility of silence. The absence of a reply is itself a trace. A blank space in a thread is more legible than a person who is physically absent.

The modern record of communication makes silence feel deliberate, even when it is not. Seen timestamps, unanswered messages, missed invitations become durable markers. Silence becomes evidence.

In public disputes, silence can be read as complicity. Not taking a position is interpreted as taking one. The person who withdraws is pulled into a binary that does not reflect the recognition that caused withdrawal in the first place.

Silence can also be read as judgment itself. When someone refuses to comment, others may assume that the refusal is a verdict, that the silence carries a superior stance.

This interpretation is common where judgment is expected. A leader who stops speaking is assumed to be disappointed. A friend who stops responding is assumed to be punishing. A colleague who stops advising is assumed to be checking out.

The person who withdraws does not control these readings. To control them would require reentering the role that is being set aside. Silence is therefore both an avoidance of false authority and an exposure to others' stories.

The exposure is costly because it can harden quickly. Once a story is shared, it gains weight. Once a story is repeated, it gains legitimacy. Silence allows stories to travel without friction.

The cost of silence is also the loss of timing. When a person speaks, they set the cadence for how a situation is framed. When they do not, others set that cadence. The frame solidifies before the silent person has a voice.

In relationships where a person was once a translator, the loss of translation is felt as disorientation. People who relied on that translation now feel unmoored. That feeling attaches itself to the person who went silent.

In some contexts, others respond to silence by escalating. They press for response. They increase the volume. They add urgency. The escalation is not merely rude. It is a bid to restore legibility.

The bid often fails. The recognition remains. The silence remains. The person who withdrew is now associated with conflict, not because they created it, but because the space they left forced it into view.

Silence can even be mistaken for calculation. A person who refuses to speak can be seen as strategic, withholding information to gain leverage. This perception is common in competitive environments where withholding is expected.

The person who withdrew may be the least strategic person in the room. Their silence may be the opposite of leverage. The social reading, however, is rarely aligned with the internal intent.

These mismatches accumulate. They produce a feeling of being misread in public. That feeling is part of the cost. It is a social cost because it changes how the person is met, invited, trusted.

That loss of control is not merely emotional. It is reputational. Reputations do not hold without reinforcement. They drift.

Reputation drift is not personal failure. It is a structural property of social memory. A reputation is a summary that must be maintained. Without new evidence, old evidence decays.

Reputation is often imagined as a stable label, but it is a moving average of recent signals. It is built from repetition and from the stories others tell about those repetitions.

When someone withdraws from visible judgment, others revise the summary. They do not hold the old version in place out of gratitude. They do not wait for the internal story. They update.

They update toward what is safe. They update toward what is legible. They update toward what is recent. Silence makes the most recent observable fact the withdrawal itself.

This produces a subtle slide. The person who was once described as clear becomes described as distant. The person who was once considered steady becomes described as unavailable.

The person who was once trusted to decide is now assumed to avoid deciding. The person who was once relied upon in conflict is now assumed to leave it where it lies.

None of this requires hostility. It can occur among people who respect each other. It can occur even among people who still care.

It is the automatic adjustment a social system makes when a signal stops repeating.

Reputation drift is especially sharp for those whose earlier roles involved judgment. They were visible because they acted. When they stop acting, they stop being legible.

A role built on judgment creates an expectation of continuity. The person becomes a reference point. When the reference point disappears, others must select a new one. The selection itself reframes the old role.

Reputational drift can feel like a slow erasure. The person's past contributions are not denied, but they become less salient. New narratives displace old ones simply because attention is finite.

This displacement can be painful. A person can feel that their history is being rewritten. The rewrite is rarely malicious. It is a way for others to make sense of the present.

People often interpret present behavior as a guide for how to read the past. When the present is withdrawal, others retrofit the past into a story of withdrawal, searching for earlier signs.

This retrofitting makes the drift feel like a judgment. It is experienced as such by the person who withdrew. But it is better understood as a shortcut in collective memory.

The social cost here is not only in how people talk. It is also about access. People rely on reputations to decide whom to involve. When a reputation becomes uncertain, people make conservative choices.

They involve someone else. They fill the gap. They route decisions around the person who has withdrawn, because uncertainty is expensive.

This is not a moral indictment. It is a resource allocation. It is a coordination move. And it means that the person who has stepped back is no longer in the same position in the network.

The cost is subtle because it appears as absence. An invitation does not arrive. A question is not asked. A project proceeds without seeking the person out. The person notices later, if at all.

The absence is the reputational cost made visible. It is the quiet loss of social centrality. People do not gather around someone whose signals have dimmed. They gather around whoever is providing the most current orientation.

Reputation drift can also be magnified by competition. When one person withdraws, others may step forward. The narrative shifts not because anyone intends harm, but because the social field rebalances itself.

In some settings, withdrawal is interpreted as a lack of competence. The recognition that authority is absent is internal. What others see is only reduced engagement. They infer lack of ability where the cause is restraint.

In other settings, withdrawal is interpreted as arrogance. A person who stops participating is seen as above the work, or uninterested in the group. The reading depends on existing myths about commitment.

These interpretations can coexist. A person can be seen as both incapable and aloof, because reputational drift operates in loose language, not in precise logic.

Reputation is also shaped by the stories people tell about themselves to others. When someone is absent, others fill in the narrative with whatever explains why they are now doing more.

That narrative often includes a gentle justification: "We had to move on." This justification is not hostile. It is a way to preserve cooperation without guilt. But it still relocates credit and influence.

The person who withdrew may feel that the group is moving on too quickly. The group may feel that it cannot wait. The mismatch is not moral. It is structural.

Reputation drift is also temporal. It accumulates over time. A brief pause can be forgiven. A sustained withdrawal becomes a new identity.

Identity is not declared. It is assigned. And once assigned, it becomes the lens through which future actions are interpreted.

A person who returns to action after a long withdrawal is read through the identity that was formed in their absence. Their action is filtered by the story already in place.

This means that the cost of not continuing can persist even after continuation resumes. The reputational drift does not reset instantly.

This can feel unfair. It can feel like being punished for honesty. But it is not a judgment. It is the inertia of social memory.

Social memory is selective. It keeps the salient. The salient is often the break, not the reasoning. The break is visible. The reasoning is not.

Reputational drift has an internal echo. A person who withdraws must live with a public version of themselves that no longer matches their private understanding. That mismatch is a quiet cost.

Reputation is not singular. It is distributed across people who know different parts of the person's history. When engagement stops, these partial reputations diverge from one another. The person who withdrew no longer supplies the shared experience that would align them.

In smaller circles, reputation is held in stories. In larger ones, it is held in shortcuts. Withdrawal reduces the flow of new story, so shortcuts carry more weight. Shortcuts are often based on prior labels and on role.

If a person was known as a fixer or stabilizer, withdrawal is read as a failure of that identity. If a person was known as a challenger, withdrawal is read as loss of courage. The role becomes a trap when the person stops performing it.

This can become self reinforcing. Because the person is now seen as less reliable, they are given fewer chances to participate. Fewer chances mean fewer signals. Fewer signals mean more drift. The loop tightens without anyone explicitly intending it.

Public settings intensify this loop. Public audiences expect a stance. They evaluate character through visible alignment. Not continuing is read as a stance anyway, usually the least charitable one. The person may be choosing restraint, but restraint looks like evasion in a public frame.

Expert roles are especially vulnerable. When an expert stops offering judgment, others question the expertise itself. The withdrawal can be read as a lack of confidence, or a lack of relevance, or a strategic dodge. The cost is a loss of authority that the person was not trying to defend in the first place.

Care roles carry their own penalties. A person who once absorbed emotion creates a sense of safety. When that absorption stops, others feel exposed, and exposure is frightening. The response is often protective distance. Distance hardens into habit.

The cost includes the future. People plan without the person. They build projects, create rituals, form routines that no longer assume that the withdrawn person will show up as before. The social future narrows.

The person may still act, but in quieter ways. Those actions can be meaningful, but they are not always legible. They do not reverse reputational drift because they are not recognized as the kind of action others were relying on.

Ambiguity is socially expensive. Groups choose clear narratives because clarity reduces friction. Withdrawal is ambiguous. It invites nuance. Nuance is rarely chosen when coordination is required. So the narrative hardens. The hardened narrative becomes the reputation.

This hardening reshapes memory. People adjust the past to align with the present. They highlight earlier moments that suggest the person was never fully committed. The adjustment is subtle, often unconscious, but it repositions the person in the shared history.

The question of action, then, is not only internal. It is a question of whether there is a socially recognizable path forward at all. Recognition does not create such a path. It only clarifies the absence of a shared authority to justify it.

This is why people who recognize absent authority often feel alone in the aftermath. They live with a private clarity that is not socially shareable.

The loneliness is not only emotional. It is structural. It comes from being positioned outside the usual circuits of judgment and response.

Yet the circuits continue. Others keep acting. They keep judging. They keep expecting. A person who withdraws is now out of rhythm with those circuits.

Out of rhythm does not mean wrong. But it does mean costly. Social systems reward synchrony. They penalize deviation, not as punishment, but as a default pattern of coordination.

This is why withdrawal can feel like misalignment.

Misalignment shows up in the smallest exchanges. Who is copied on a message, who is asked to weigh in, who is trusted to make a call. These micro exclusions are rarely announced. They accumulate quietly until the person feels less central than before.

Others adjust in the name of ease. They route around the uncertainty by choosing people who respond in familiar ways. The withdrawn person becomes someone to manage around, not because of hostility, but because of predictability. Ease replaces depth.

The cost is not only lost influence. It is lost ease. A person who once moved naturally within a group now feels slightly out of step. That friction is social. It changes how often people reach out, and how often the person responds.

Even when it is ethically coherent, it is socially awkward. It creates friction. It requires others to adjust.

Adjustment is work. Work creates resentment. Resentment reshapes memory. Memory reshapes reputation. This loop is the cost.

The person who withdraws may see only a boundary. The group sees a disruption. The group may interpret the disruption as a statement about the group itself.

The disruption can be read as criticism, or as superiority, or as a refusal to share burden. Even when none of these are intended, this is how group narratives work.

The social cost therefore includes misinterpretation. Misinterpretation is not accidental. It is the natural outcome of incomplete information.

Incomplete information is not easily corrected, because correction requires reengaging the role that was abandoned. That reengagement can feel like a betrayal of the recognition.

So the cost sits. It sits in the space between private clarity and public narrative. It sits in the subtle reordering of ties.

Relationships are structured around expectations. Not continuing alters expectations. It changes what can be asked, what can be assumed, what can be counted on.

Expectations are not only about tasks. They are about availability. A person who once held uncertainty for others is expected to keep doing so. When they stop, others feel less held, less oriented.

Recalibration often includes role substitution. Someone else becomes the voice of clarity. Someone else becomes the informal judge. The previous holder of that role becomes an observer. The shift changes power, not by decree, but by usage.

New alignments form around the new sources of clarity. People gather where they can predict a response. The withdrawn person is not necessarily excluded. They are simply less necessary. The cost is this quiet demotion.

Over time, participation becomes ritualized. Invitations follow habit. Habit follows proximity and recent engagement. A person who has stepped back is invited to fewer decisions, more social surfaces, less of the inner work.

In close relationships, recalibration looks like caution. People share less because they expect less return. They stop bringing dilemmas because they no longer expect help. The bond thins without a clear break.

Recalibration also touches identity. If a person has long been valued for judgment, withdrawal removes the mirror that reflected that value. The social world stops confirming an important part of who they were.

This produces a feedback loop. Fewer invitations lead to less participation. Less participation confirms that the person is no longer central to the group's movement. The loop feels personal, but it is systemic.

Recalibration can resemble grief. People mourn a version of the person who used to be available in a certain way. There is no ceremony for this loss, no clear moment when it happens. The ambiguity makes the loss harder to name, but not less real.

Because there is no clear ending, people create their own closure. They tell themselves that the person has moved on, that the relationship has changed, that a previous chapter has closed. That story provides relief, but it also fixes distance in place.

The withdrawn person may still be present, which complicates the story. Presence without the old role feels like a reminder of what is gone. Others become cautious, avoiding topics that once felt safe. The relationship becomes polite, not because care vanished, but because the old confidence did.

Replacement makes the change feel permanent. When another person takes up the old function, the difference in style turns the old role into history. The withdrawal is no longer a pause. It becomes a new normal that others internalize.

These changes can be invisible to outsiders. There may be no conflict, no dramatic break. The cost is quiet erosion. It is felt in the shrinking of shared space and in the silence around what used to be shared.

The loop is not punishment. It is coordination. People align with those who provide consistent engagement. Those who step back become harder to align around, so alignment shifts elsewhere.

There are moments when this recalibration becomes visible. A crisis occurs, and the person is not called. A decision is made, and their absence is noticed. The cost is felt as an absence of trust, even when trust was never broken.

The result is a remapped social field. The person becomes a known absence, a familiar silence, a presence that is no longer structural to how the group moves.

Sometimes this recalibration is made explicit, through a conversation, through a role change, through a formal shift. More often it is implicit. It happens in the texture of everyday interaction.

People stop asking for opinions. They stop testing ideas. They stop seeking mediation. They stop turning toward someone who once held those responsibilities.

That shift can feel like relief for everyone involved. It can also feel like loss. It can be read as rejection, or as freedom, or as disrespect. Sometimes it is all at once.

The social cost of not continuing is not only in the loss of influence. It is also in the loss of intimacy. Intimacy is built on participation. Withdrawing from judgment often means withdrawing from shared interpretation.

Shared interpretation is a bond. It is how two people create a private language about what is happening. When one person stops contributing, the language thins.

The thinning is not always obvious. It may look like fewer conversations, shorter replies, longer pauses. It may look like silence.

People often interpret this thinning as a change of heart. They may assume that the bond has weakened or that trust is lost. They may assume that what is really lost is attention or care.

The person who has withdrawn may experience something different. The internal story is not about care or disdain. It is about authority. It is about the recognition that judgment is no longer owned or shareable.

This is one of the most painful gaps in the social cost. The internal story is often about honesty. The external reading is often about motivation. The two do not meet.

Not continuing is therefore not just a private decision. It is a relational event. It reorganizes how people read each other. It reorganizes how much interpretation they are willing to do.

In many settings, continuity is treated as respect. A person who keeps showing up, keeps engaging, keeps taking a stand, is experienced as loyal.

When that person stops, others can feel devalued. They might think that the relationship was conditional, that involvement was merely instrumental.

This sense of devaluation is not always accurate. But it is socially real. It affects how people respond. It affects how much they extend themselves in return.

The social cost also appears in the way communities manage uncertainty. When someone steps back, others are forced to absorb more ambiguity.

Some people welcome that ambiguity. Others are alarmed by it. The alarm can turn into pressure, explicit or implicit, for the person to return and take up the old role.

The pressure is rarely framed as a demand for authority. It is framed as a request for help, for clarity, for steadiness.

This framing makes the cost more difficult to name. The person who withdraws can look unhelpful, while the person who requests can look reasonable.

The asymmetry is structural. Those who remain in the flow experience a deficit. Those who step out experience a boundary. The boundary is invisible without the internal story.

That invisibility creates interpretive noise. It creates stories that the person who withdrew cannot correct without reentering the role.

Reentering the role may be impossible without pretending authority. So the stories remain. They thicken. They circulate.

The social cost here is not only rumor. It is the erosion of trust in the person's reliability as a participant.

Trust is not only about what a person believes. It is about what a person will do when asked. Withdrawal changes that expectation.

Some relationships survive the change easily. Others do not. Those that survive are often those with wider foundations. But even there, the texture shifts.

The shift can be subtle. A friend may still care but stop seeking advice. A colleague may still respect but stop involving. A family member may still love but stop confiding.

These shifts are not always deliberate. They are adaptations. They are social recalibrations made without ceremony.

From the inside, this can feel like loss without a visible rupture. It can feel like being present but slightly out of phase with the group.

There is also a moral layer. Many cultures treat action as evidence of character. Decisiveness is celebrated. Inaction is suspect.

When someone stops acting, the moral story shifts. People ask not only what happened, but what kind of person would stop.

This is one reason why not continuing is costly. It is not only a practical withdrawal. It is a perceived shift in character.

The person who recognizes that judgment authority is absent does not control this moral interpretation. The recognition is private. The moral reading is public.

Public readings are shaped by shared narratives about duty, responsibility, and care. Withdrawal is easily framed as avoidance of duty, withdrawal of care.

Even in settings that value boundaries and humility, continuity is still expected. The person who withdraws may be praised for integrity and still be kept at distance.

This is not hypocrisy. It is the coexistence of two norms. Integrity is admired. Reliability is required. The person who withdraws satisfies one and violates the other.

The social cost is the space between admiration and reliance. It is the gap where people respect the person but no longer involve them.

In organizations, this gap can harden quickly. Performance systems assume continuity. A person who withdraws from visible judgment can be marked as stagnant, regardless of the private clarity that motivated the withdrawal.

The marking may be subtle. Fewer invitations. Less visibility. Less urgency in feedback. It may not be punitive, but it accumulates.

In families, where roles are sticky, withdrawal can be read as a rejection of kinship. People may feel that the person has refused their place.

That reading can lead to distance, retaliation, or quiet grief. The person who withdraws may be confused by the intensity, but the intensity is a response to altered expectation.

In friendships, withdrawal can be read as a shift in priorities. The social cost is not only less contact, but a revised story about where one stands.

These revised stories can be hard to reverse, not because people are stubborn, but because relationships are built on lived experience more than on explanation.

A person who has withdrawn may try to explain. But explanation itself can sound like a renewed claim to authority, or like a defense. It can reopen the very role that was being set down.

So explanation is often withheld. The silence continues. The cost continues. This is one reason why withdrawal feels like a one-way door in social life.

The cost is not uniform. It varies with status. A high status person can withdraw and remain legible. A lower status person can withdraw and disappear.

Status provides a cushion. It preserves a reputation through silence. Without status, silence is interpreted as absence of value.

The person who withdraws is not necessarily seeking silence. They are seeking accuracy. But accuracy does not always read as value.

This is a second asymmetry. Accuracy is internal. Value is external. When they diverge, people choose the external reading.

The social cost is also temporal. It accumulates over time. A brief pause can be forgiven. A sustained withdrawal becomes a new identity.

Identity is not declared. It is assigned. And once assigned, it becomes the lens through which future actions are interpreted.

A person who returns to action after a long withdrawal is read through the identity that was formed in their absence. Their action is filtered by the story already in place.

This means that the cost of not continuing can persist even after continuation resumes. The reputational drift does not reset instantly.

This can feel unfair. It can feel like being punished for honesty. But it is not a judgment. It is the inertia of social memory.

Social memory is selective. It keeps the salient. The salient is often the break, not the reasoning. The break is visible. The reasoning is not.

This is why people who recognize absent authority often feel alone in the aftermath. They live with a private clarity that is not socially shareable.

The loneliness is not only emotional. It is structural. It comes from being positioned outside the usual circuits of judgment and response.

Yet the circuits continue. Others keep acting. They keep judging. They keep expecting. A person who withdraws is now out of rhythm with those circuits.

Out of rhythm does not mean wrong. But it does mean costly. Social systems reward synchrony. They penalize deviation, not as punishment, but as a default pattern of coordination.

This is why withdrawal can feel like misalignment.

Misalignment shows up in the smallest exchanges. Who is copied on a message, who is asked to weigh in, who is trusted to make a call. These micro exclusions are rarely announced. They accumulate quietly until the person feels less central than before.

Others adjust in the name of ease. They route around the uncertainty by choosing people who respond in familiar ways. The withdrawn person becomes someone to manage around, not because of hostility, but because of predictability. Ease replaces depth.

The cost is not only lost influence. It is lost ease. A person who once moved naturally within a group now feels slightly out of step. That friction is social. It changes how often people reach out, and how often the person responds.

Even when it is ethically coherent, it is socially awkward. It creates friction. It requires others to adjust.

Adjustment is work. Work creates resentment. Resentment reshapes memory. Memory reshapes reputation. This loop is the cost.

The person who withdraws may see only a boundary. The group sees a disruption. The group may interpret the disruption as a statement about the group itself.

The disruption can be read as criticism, or as superiority, or as a refusal to share burden. Even when none of these are intended, this is how group narratives work.

The social cost therefore includes misinterpretation. Misinterpretation is not accidental. It is the natural outcome of incomplete information.

Incomplete information is not easily corrected, because correction requires reengaging the role that was abandoned. That reengagement can feel like a betrayal of the recognition.

So the cost sits. It sits in the space between private clarity and public narrative. It sits in the subtle reordering of ties.

The cost also sits in the observer. People who relied on the person must now absorb uncertainty. They may feel exposed. They may feel unprotected. They may compensate by closing ranks or hardening rules.

Those compensations can further push the withdrawn person away. A system that tightens does not easily make room for someone who has stepped back.

This can create a cycle. Withdrawal leads to tightening. Tightening makes reentry harder. Reentry failure confirms the story that the person is gone.

Again, this is not an intentional punishment. It is the path of least resistance in social coordination. It is how groups avoid chaos.

The social cost of not continuing is therefore not merely about a single person. It is about the system that treats continuity as proof of commitment.

There is a final irony. Sometimes the person who withdraws is respected for honesty, while also being avoided for uncertainty. The respect does not remove the cost. It only makes the cost harder to name.

It is possible to recognize that a person was right to withdraw and still feel abandoned. It is possible to admire their restraint and still choose to work with someone else.

These mixed responses are part of the social cost. They reveal how plural social evaluation really is. One dimension can praise what another dimension penalizes.

This is why the absence of judgment authority is not the end of social stakes. It does not cancel expectation. It does not erase obligation. It does not protect the person from how others update.

The person who does not continue does not escape the social field. They remain within it, now reframed. The field is less interested in why than in what. The what is silence, withdrawal, nonparticipation.

Observers often ask whether the withdrawal helped, whether it was worth it, whether anything improved. Those questions assume that the situation was fixable and that action would have produced a measurable result. Recognition does not guarantee that.

Without a shared metric, comparison collapses. Advice loses traction. One person's restraint looks like another person's failure. The social world tends to fill this ambiguity with evaluation, because evaluation is easier than admitting that no clear measure exists.

Action after recognition is often situational. It is not justified by obligation. It is justified by local necessity, by immediate constraints, by the smallest workable aim. From the outside, this looks inconsistent, because the consistency that others expect depends on a shared authority.

When the authority is absent, consistency becomes private. It is held inside the person rather than between people. That privateness looks like arbitrariness, not because it is arbitrary, but because the logic is not legible to others.

Quiet action can still occur. It often does. But it is less performative, less urgent, less oriented toward proof. The quietness protects the person from false claims, while also reducing how visible the action is. The social cost remains.

Many people continue acting precisely to avoid that cost. They keep providing judgment because the social penalty of withholding feels too large. This does not make their action more legitimate. It makes their position more socially sustainable.

The cost can feel like a tax on integrity. To refuse a false authority is to accept misunderstanding. The misunderstanding is not a simple mistake. It is the natural price of being out of sync with a system that values continuous signal.

Explanation rarely resolves this. To explain is to reenter the role that was set aside. It is to offer a new judgment about why judgment was absent. That circularity is part of why silence persists, and why its cost accumulates.

The tension is the reality. Recognition provides clarity. It does not provide refuge. It does not offer a socially shared shelter from expectation. The person who withdraws remains exposed to the readings of others.

What looks like inaction is a real response. What looks like absence is a real position. The social world may not accept it, but it cannot make it disappear. The cost is the price of that irreconcilable difference.

The cost is the price of that reframing. It is the fading of a role, the drift of a reputation, the recalibration of ties. It is the misunderstanding that sits where explanation cannot.

Nothing dramatic follows. And that is not a failure. It is the point.

Chapter 11

The necessary blank

After everything has been seen, something remains undone.

What remains is not a task that was forgotten, and not a final piece that slipped away, but a residue that cannot be pressed into a task at all. It feels like the ending has stopped short, yet the shortness is not an error. It is the shape of the boundary that has been drawn throughout the book, now visible because nothing else is left to cover it.

This is often perceived as a problem.

The reading mind is trained to expect release, trained to look for the line that converts insight into instruction, trained to treat a final chapter as a hinge that swings into action or certainty. When that hinge is missing, what appears first is a sense of malfunction, as if the book has failed to complete its own design. The blank is felt before it is understood. It reads like an absence of care, a refusal to finish the work, a failure to do the last courtesy.

A missing conclusion. An unfinished argument. A lack of closure.

These labels arrive quickly because they are the usual names for the discomfort that follows a stopping point without resolution. They assume that the proper state of a text is a completed cycle, that the reader should be escorted out by a final set of sentences that tell the meaning of everything that came before. When those sentences do not arrive, the mind reaches for familiar diagnoses, as if naming the lack will allow it to be mended. Yet the lack does not want mending, and the naming does not help, because the lack is not a defect. It is a deliberate non-transfer.

But the absence here is not accidental.

It is structural.

The blank is not a gap in information but a structural refusal to provide a position that would not belong to the author to provide. Structural does not mean abstract. It means the absence is part of the frame, part of the internal logic that makes the book the kind of object it is. It means that even if more words were added, the blank would remain, not because it is hidden, but because it is the border of what the book can do.

If judgment authority cannot be transferred, then no final position can be handed over.

The conclusion in most texts is a transfer mechanism. It tries to carry the reader from description to stance, from a collection of observations to a shared posture toward the world. That posture may be described as insight, or as recommendation, or as moral clarity, but in every case it functions as a handoff. A final position is not only an idea, it is an assignment of where to stand. If the authority to stand there cannot be transferred, then the final position itself would be an overreach. The book can say what it has seen, but it cannot assign what must be carried.

Any attempt to conclude on behalf of the reader would violate the very boundary this book describes.

The boundary is not a statement about modesty. It is not a confession of weakness, and not a gesture of politeness. It is a structural limit on substitution. To conclude on behalf of the reader would be to pretend that the book can take the place of the reader's own situated authority, that a general voice can speak as if it bore the particular consequences that the reader bears. That is precisely the substitution that the rest of the book has refused. So the refusal appears here as an ending without closure.

So the book stops before resolution.

Stopping is not the same as finishing. Stopping leaves something visible that finishing would conceal. Finishing would smooth the edge, turning the boundary into a summary, turning the remaining ambiguity into a decision, turning the reader's discomfort into a product. Stopping does not resolve the discomfort. It lets the discomfort remain in view as part of the subject itself. The book ends by not ending, which is the only way to keep faith with what it has claimed.

This is not humility. It is constraint.

Humility can be performed. It can be announced, or used to soften the authority that nonetheless remains intact. Constraint is different. It is not a posture but a limit. The author is not choosing to step back out of modesty. The author is unable to step forward without crossing the boundary that the book has drawn. Constraint means there is no permissible sentence that can do the usual work of a conclusion without erasing the central claim.

Many systems depend on closure to stabilize meaning.

Stories end. Lessons crystallize. Frameworks resolve into rules.

Closure makes the world feel handleable. It delivers a feeling of completion that allows the reader to move on without carrying uncertainty. In institutions, closure is also a way of distributing responsibility. When a policy is concluded, when a report ends with recommendations, when a narrative finishes with a moral, responsibility is carried forward as a package that can be handed to the next person. The system can proceed because the meaning has been fixed enough to transmit. The blank in this chapter refuses that fix.

Judgment Authority does not behave like that.

It resists crystallization. It does not harden into rules that can be applied without remainder. Judgment Authority is tied to location, to the particular stakes and consequences that cannot be lifted out and passed around without changing what they are. That is why it does not close. Closure would require detachment, and detachment would transform judgment into a formula. What the book insists on is precisely the non-formula nature of judgment authority, its refusal to be made portable.

Once seen, it cannot be unseen.

But it also cannot be completed.

Seeing here is not a single epiphany. It is a recognition of how authority operates when it is assigned and when it is inferred, how responsibility is carried without being named, and how closure can be used to disguise the transfer of burdens. Once that recognition appears, it does not return to invisibility. Yet recognition is not completion. It does not settle into a final state. It continues to be unfinished because what it recognizes is unfinished. The boundary is not a step on the way. It is the edge itself.

Readers often report a strange sensation at this point.

Not confusion. Not frustration.

But suspension.

Suspension is the feeling of being held in a space that is clear enough to be inhabited but not resolved enough to be released. It can feel like a pause that is longer than expected, a pause that does not reveal what it is pausing for. Suspension is a form of clarity that does not condense into instruction. It is the experience of understanding without the comfort of a next move. That discomfort is not a failure of comprehension. It is a signal that the book has held to its constraint.

The sense that something has shifted permanently, without producing instruction.

A shift without instruction is destabilizing in a culture that expects insight to be usable. Many readers are trained to convert recognition into tools, steps, or frameworks. But the shift described here does not convert. It sits in the reader as a change in perception, a heightened awareness of where authority is real and where it is presumed, without a corresponding map for how to act. That map would be a transfer. Its absence preserves the integrity of the recognition itself.

This is the correct outcome.

Correct here does not mean satisfying. It means faithful to the boundary. The outcome is correct because it refuses to violate the premise on which the book stands. A more satisfying outcome would have been easier to sell, more compatible with the expectations that follow a final chapter, more likely to be remembered as advice. But that satisfaction would rest on a betrayal. The correct outcome keeps the betrayal from occurring, which means it must also keep the discomfort alive.

What follows this book is not a practice.

It is not a method.

It is not an identity.

The book is not meant to become a routine that can be repeated, or a method that can be taught, or a badge that can be worn. To let it become any of those would be to make it transferable in the very way it refuses. The text does not offer a program for how to live with judgment authority. It only insists that judgment authority cannot be given away. The absence of a program is not a lack of generosity. It is the only way to avoid replacing one form of transfer with another.

It is a sensitivity.

Sensitivity is quieter than method. It does not announce itself, and it cannot be easily displayed. It is a shift in the way situations are perceived and felt, an attunement to moments when responsibility is being allocated without being spoken. It is a sensitivity to the pull of closure, to the relief that comes when ambiguity is reduced, and to the costs that often follow that relief. Sensitivity does not command action. It simply changes what can be noticed.

A reduced willingness to carry outcomes that were never assigned.

This line is not a directive. It names a tendency that appears when the boundary is recognized. Often the burden of outcomes is carried by default, not because it was given, but because someone had to carry it, and the person with the most capacity, or the most quietness, or the most tolerance was expected to absorb it. Reduced willingness does not look like refusal so much as a recalibration of what belongs to whom. It is a subtle disturbance in the usual flow of assumed responsibility. The disturbance is not a rule. It is a consequence of seeing.

A refusal to finalize what remains structurally open.

Finalization is attractive because it provides the feeling of completion. But there are matters that do not belong to completion, matters whose open nature is part of their truth. The refusal described here is not stubbornness. It is a recognition that some things can only be made final by flattening their reality. Structural openness cannot be solved without pretending it was accidental. The refusal is the maintenance of honesty.

An increased tolerance for situations that do not converge.

Non-convergence is a feature of many situations, not a temporary phase. Projects stall, relationships circle, institutions delay, not always because of negligence but because the issues themselves do not resolve into a single line. Tolerance here means the ability to remain present to this reality without fabricating a solution. It is not indifference. It is a steadiness in the face of conditions that do not answer to pressure.

Nothing needs to be done with this.

The recognition does not require a transformation into activity. It does not need to be translated into a checklist, or into a new way of speaking, or into a set of habits. To demand that it be turned into action would again be to force a transfer, to make the book serve as a tool for producing outcomes. The blank disallows that demand. It stays as a limit, visible and quiet.

It will appear on its own.

In meetings. In relationships. In projects. In silence.

It appears in ordinary life as a subtle pause, a sense that an explanation is being offered too quickly, or that a decision is being framed as if it belonged to someone else. The appearance is not dramatic. It is often a feeling that arrives after the words, a recognition that the exchange has drifted into assumption. Sometimes the appearance is quiet, so quiet that it only registers later, when the moment has passed and the line of responsibility looks different than it did at the time.

You will notice when explanation begins to feel dishonest.

Dishonest explanation is not always false. It can be accurate in its details and still feel dishonest because it is being used to close a space that cannot be closed. The dishonesty is in the gesture, not necessarily in the facts. It is the gesture that says, here is the answer, when the real condition is, here is the boundary. The reader who has seen the boundary feels the dishonesty even when the explanation is correct.

You will notice when effort becomes compensatory.

Compensatory effort is effort that tries to make up for the lack of authority, for the absence of a rightful decision. It can appear as extra work, or as a rush to fix, or as a flood of carefulness meant to protect against criticism. The effort is real, and may even be admirable, but its role is to compensate for a lack that cannot be repaired by more effort. Noticing this does not produce a solution. It produces a sharper sense of what effort can and cannot cover.

You will notice when responsibility is being inferred, not given.

Inference happens in the spaces where authority has not been assigned. Someone speaks as if a decision has already been made. Silence is interpreted as consent. Urgency is used as a reason to assume a burden. These are not rare dynamics. They are woven into the fabric of how groups function. What changes after this book is not that the dynamics disappear, but that they become harder to ignore. The inference is seen as inference, not as a fact.

And sometimes, you will do nothing.

Doing nothing here is not apathy. It is not laziness, and not a refusal to engage. It is the recognition that no action can be taken in the name of a judgment that has not been granted. Doing nothing is not the same as doing nothing forever. It is a way the boundary shows itself in a given moment, a moment that does not belong to the reader's authority. The stillness is temporary, but it is also precise.

Not because you are unsure.

But because there is nothing there to resolve.

Uncertainty is a lack of knowledge that can sometimes be filled. The condition described here is not a lack of knowledge. It is the presence of a boundary that remains even when the facts are clear. The facts do not grant authority. They make the scene visible, but they do not give the right to complete it. So the lack of resolution does not come from confusion. It comes from clarity about what cannot be completed.

This book does not tell you what to decide.

It shows you when deciding was never yours.

The showing is not a directive. It is a description of the edges where responsibility shifts. It names how often a decision is taken because it can be, not because it should be. It describes the habit of stepping into the empty space and calling it leadership, when the space is empty because no one has been granted the authority to fill it. The book does not reject decision. It rejects the false assignment of decision.

The blank that remains is not a gap.

It is the boundary itself.

It is the line that cannot be crossed without falsehood, visible only because the usual signals of closure have been withheld. In that visibility, the blank becomes a presence, not a void. It carries a weight that is not easy to name, a weight that comes from the knowledge that there is no final word here that can be given without disguise.

The remaining blank is also a mirror. It reflects the reader's desire for completion, for a sense that the work is finished and the meaning has been secured. That desire is not a flaw. It is a normal response to the way reading is usually structured. The mirror does not condemn the desire. It simply makes it visible, so that the book cannot be mistaken for a substitute authority. The mirror remains even after the page is turned.

The authorial refusal to close can be mistaken for evasion, as if the author were hiding behind ambiguity. But refusal is not the same as evasion. Evasion avoids responsibility. Refusal here is a way of respecting the responsibility that cannot be taken. It is an insistence that some claims cannot be made without taking what is not owned. The book refuses to take it. That refusal does not feel like warmth. It feels like a blank.

Reader discomfort is part of the text, not a side effect. It is the sensation that signals the limit has been reached. Discomfort here is not meant to be cured, because curing it would require a closure that the book cannot provide. The discomfort is the shape of the reader's contact with the boundary. It is not a punishment. It is an honest consequence of the claims that have been made.

Absence is usually taken as evidence of neglect. But some absences are deliberate, a necessary space left open because to fill it would distort what it names. The absence in this chapter is not a lack of care, but a sign of care for the integrity of judgment. It is an absence that protects what cannot be protected by any other means.

The blank is also a form of witness. It witnesses the limits of language to carry authority. Language can describe, can narrate, can explain, can persuade. But language cannot bestow the right to bear consequences that belong to another person. The blank is the point where language stops trying to do what it cannot do. It is the point where the text stands beside the reader without stepping into the reader's place.

In most books, the ending is the place where the author stands tallest, where the voice becomes most confident, where the reader is told what it all meant. Here the ending is the place where the author steps back, not out of uncertainty, but out of accuracy. The step back is not humility. It is fidelity to the claim that authority is not portable. The text becomes quieter because it has reached its limit.

The limit is not the edge of knowledge. It is the edge of transfer. Knowledge can be transmitted, explained, taught. But authority over judgment is not the same as knowledge. It is tied to consequence, which cannot be transported without changing its owner. That is why the book can say much and still stop where it stops. It is why the ending feels like an unfinished thought even though it is complete in its own terms.

An unresolved ending is often taken as a failure of craft. But in this case the craft is in the refusal to resolve. The writer is not leaving the reader with a puzzle to solve. The writer is leaving the reader with a boundary that cannot be solved. The craft is in holding that boundary visible without covering it. That is a different kind of ending, one that does not collapse the space between author and reader.

The blank does not wait for the reader to fill it. It does not invite completion. It resists it. The blank remains because the book is not a tool for delegating judgment. If the reader tries to fill it, what appears is not completion but substitution, a filling that uses the book as if it

318

had granted permission. The refusal of the blank is a refusal of that permission.

This is why the ending can feel almost unsatisfying, like a conversation that stops before the last sentence. The missing sentence is not missing because the author could not find it. It is missing because any sentence that would close the conversation would speak beyond the author's right. The unsatisfaction is not an error. It is the evidence that the boundary is still intact.

The experience is similar to standing at the edge of a map. Maps are drawn to be used. They end where the territory has not been charted. The blank margin does not mean nothing exists there. It means the map ends. The map cannot tell you what lies beyond the edge, and any claim that it does would be a claim about authority, not about geography. The blank here is the map's edge, visible because the book stops.

The blank also exposes the reader's relationship to the author. Readers are often willing to accept instructions because they believe the author has carried the responsibility for those instructions. When the author refuses to carry it, that relationship shifts. The reader is not abandoned, but neither is the reader led. The relationship becomes a proximity rather than a transfer. It is a different kind of trust, one that accepts the boundary instead of demanding a conclusion.

This chapter does not undo what has been said before. It demonstrates it. The blank is the demonstration. If judgment authority cannot be transferred, then the chapter cannot do what a normal final chapter does. The demonstration is not a proof in the traditional sense. It is a practical enactment of the claim, visible in the book's own ending. This is the point where argument becomes form.

The blank is sometimes mistaken for a lack of care for the reader's experience. But care can take the form of restraint. To restrain the desire to conclude is to respect the reader's position as the only one who can carry their own authority. The reader is not given a conclusion because the reader's conclusion cannot be given. The restraint is not cold. It is a form of fidelity.

There is also a quiet honesty in refusing closure. Closure can be honest when the subject itself closes. But in matters where authority cannot be transferred, closure is a form of fiction. It is the fiction that a general statement can replace a specific stance. The book declines to offer that fiction. The refusal is a way of saying that the truth here is the absence, not a final statement that pretends to resolve it.

The reader discomfort is often a signal that the reader expects to be told what to do. That expectation is not wrong. It is the normal contract between books and readers in many domains. The contract is broken here because the book refuses to make the transfer. The discomfort is the sound of the contract tearing. It is also the sound of the boundary being respected.

The authorial refusal to close is also a refusal to monetize the reader's attention through certainty. Certainty is a commodity. It can be sold as assurance, as a solution, as a guide. The refusal to conclude refuses to sell that commodity in a case where it would be counterfeit. The blank is a refusal to convert recognition into a product. It is a refusal to trade in borrowed authority.

The blank has no instruction because instruction would imply that the author can judge on behalf of the reader. Instruction is a form of authority. It presumes a right to direct the reader's action. That right is not present here. The author can only describe what judgment authority is, not exercise it for another. The absence of instruction is the form of that restraint. It is the only ending that fits the premise.

There is a subtle difference between leaving the reader and leaving the reader alone. The book does not abandon. It simply refuses to take over. Abandonment would be the absence of care. Refusal is a different act. It is the act of not substituting for what cannot be substituted. The book stays near the reader by keeping the boundary visible, by acknowledging what it cannot do. It stops at the edge and remains there.

The blank is not a lesson. Lessons are meant to be carried into future situations. They are a way of compressing experience into a portable rule. This book has refused that portability. The blank therefore refuses to become a lesson. It remains tied to the recognition that judgment cannot be packaged. If it were turned into a lesson, its core claim would be undone.

The absence also resists the desire to be useful. Usefulness is often equated with action and application. But usefulness in this context would mean giving the reader something to do with the recognition. That would be a transfer. The book chooses not to be useful in that way. It chooses to be accurate. Accuracy here looks like refusal. It looks like a blank.

The blank does not settle into a moral. A moral is a way of telling a reader what to take away, what to remember, what to apply. A moral can be comforting because it reduces the complexity of a story into a single line. The blank denies that reduction. It keeps the complexity intact by refusing to collapse it into a portable message. The reader leaves without a moral because the subject does not permit one.

The ending is also a test of the reader's appetite for transfer. Not a test in the sense of evaluation, but a test in the sense of revealing what the reader seeks. Some readers will desire a final position, and their desire will be clear in the discomfort they feel. Others will find the blank familiar, recognizing it as the shape of situations that never close. In both cases the blank is honest. It shows what it shows without trying to manage the result.

The blank is a form of silence. Silence here is not the absence of speech but the presence of a boundary in speech. It is the silence of a sentence that could be written but should not be. It is the silence that holds when the only available words would overstep. This kind of silence is not empty. It is full of restraint, full of the recognition that authority is not transferable. The silence is the final line.

The reader may feel that the book has stopped too early. That feeling is accurate if measured against normal expectations. The book does stop early by the standards of closure. But it does not stop early by the standards of its own claim. It stops exactly where it must to avoid saying what it cannot say. The early stop is not an accident. It is the only place where the book can end truthfully.

The blank can be misread as a gap in courage, as if the author were unwilling to stand behind a claim. But the author has already stood behind the claim that authority cannot be transferred. To stand behind a conclusion would be to contradict that claim. Courage here is not the courage of asserting a final answer. It is the courage of stopping. The blank is a courage of restraint.

The chapter role is unresolved ending, not as a stylistic trick but as a necessity. An unresolved ending is not a cliffhanger. It does not promise a sequel. It does not tease a resolution that will appear later. It is simply unresolved. It stays where it is, without the promise that it will be tied off elsewhere. The absence is final in the sense that it will not be filled, but it is not final in the sense of closure.

A refusal to close is also a refusal to summarize what has been said in a way that would compress its meaning into a formula. Summaries are useful because they allow a reader to carry something forward. But a summary here would be a substitute for judgment. It would be an attempt to carry the weight in a portable form. The book declines to produce that portable weight. It ends in place, not in summary.

The blank is not only for the reader. It is also for the author. The author is not exempt from the boundary. The author cannot step beyond it without betraying the same rule. To leave the ending open is to accept the limit on authorial authority as well. It acknowledges that the writer is not a judge over the reader's circumstances. The blank is the author's boundary too.

The absence is a kind of respect. Respect is often imagined as approval or guidance. Here it takes the form of not taking the reader's place. It is respect for the reader's capacity and for the reader's burden. The author does not offer to carry that burden, because to offer it would be to claim a right that does not exist. Respect in this case is restraint, not advice.

The blank holds the reader in a space between insight and action, not as a trap but as a faithful reflection of how judgment authority operates. Action outside authority structure is not the action the book can authorize. The book is clear on what it can do, and clear on what it cannot. That clarity is the content of the blank. It is the reason the blank exists, and the reason it must remain.

The necessary blank is also a reminder that the book is not complete in the way a manual is complete. A manual ends with steps. A manual can be finished because it offers a procedure. This book does not offer a procedure. It offers a recognition. Recognition is not completed by being turned into steps. It remains what it is. The blank honors that.

Because there is no transfer, there is no resolution that can be owned by the author. The author can say that the ending is unresolved, can explain why, can describe the discomfort, can name the boundary, but cannot give the reader what a conclusion usually gives. The most honest closing line is the one that does not close, that lets the boundary remain visible. That is the reason for the necessary blank.

The blank is not a void that demands to be filled. It is a line that cannot be crossed. It is an ending that keeps the premise intact by refusing the comfort of resolution. It leaves the reader with a clear view of the boundary and nothing else. The ending does not soften this. It does not apologize. It remains where it is.

The necessary blank does not provide peace. It provides accuracy. Peace would be the feeling that everything has been resolved, that the reader can move on with a new set of instructions. Accuracy is the feeling that the boundary has been honored. It is less soothing and more exact. It does not promise relief. It simply stays true.

The word necessary in the title does not refer to a choice. It is not necessary in the sense that it is useful, or necessary in the sense that it accomplishes something. It is necessary because the boundary cannot be crossed without converting judgment into something it is not. If a conclusion were provided, the entire claim of the book would become incoherent, because the conclusion would be the very transfer the text has refused. Necessity here is structural, not practical. The blank exists because the book cannot exist without it.

Absence is sometimes confused with permission. It can look like an empty space that invites any filling. But the blank here does not authorize arbitrary filling. It is not a license. It is a restraint. It narrows the possibilities by insisting that the author will not stand in for the reader, and it leaves the reader with the recognition that the author cannot validate whatever choice might follow. The blank does not widen the field. It marks the edge.

In some traditions of reading, the end of a book is expected to deliver a distilled line, a saying that can be remembered, quoted, repeated. Such lines are portable, and portability is their value. This chapter refuses to produce that kind of line. There is nothing at the end that can be lifted out and used as a principle without altering its meaning. The refusal is not accidental. It is the way the book prevents its own capture as doctrine.

The absence of examples is part of the same restraint. Examples are attractive because they make abstraction concrete. But examples also become templates. They invite transfer. They suggest that the contours of one situation can be applied to another. Here the avoidance of examples is not a failure of generosity. It is a refusal to turn the boundary into a pattern. The book chooses to remain at the level where judgment authority cannot be borrowed.

Time does not close the blank. If anything, time can make it more visible. The reader may finish the chapter and find the sensation returning later, not as a remembered sentence but as a persistent gap where a directive might have been. The memory of the book is not a memory of advice. It is a memory of a line that refused to be crossed. That memory is less crisp than a quotation, but more durable as a presence.

Much of modern discourse is oriented toward deliverables, toward outcomes that can be tracked and repeated. The book stands against that orientation without offering an alternative that can be packaged. It accepts the possibility that not all forms of understanding produce deliverables. This is not a romantic view of uncertainty. It is a recognition that some forms of authority cannot be made into output without distortion. The blank is the place where that distortion is refused.

There is a distinction between expertise and authority that becomes visible here. Expertise can often be transmitted. It can be taught, tested, certified, carried from one context into another. Authority over judgment is not the same. It belongs to those who bear the consequences, and it cannot be detached from that burden without becoming theater. The blank is the marker of that distinction. It does not diminish expertise. It simply refuses to mistake expertise for authority.

The refusal to close also resists the way books are often used as instruments of reassurance. Reassurance is a form of closure. It tells the reader that the uncertainty has been contained. But in this case the uncertainty is not accidental. It is the shape of the truth. To reassure would be to lie. The book chooses to leave the uncertainty intact, because the integrity of judgment authority demands it.

Silence at the end is not a void. It is a counterweight to the abundance of explanation that comes before it. The silence acknowledges that explanation has limits, that there is a point where adding more words would only add more substitution. The silence is not meant to be interpreted as mystical. It is practical. It is the limit of what can be said without trespassing. The blank is that silence made visible.

An unresolved ending often implies that another ending is hidden somewhere else, that a later chapter, another book, a future conversation will provide the missing closure. Here there is no promise of such a later closure. The unresolved ending is not a hint. It is not a teaser. It is an ending that refuses to become anything else. The blank does not wait for a sequel. It simply remains.

The reader may notice that the book has been analytical, careful to name what it sees, and yet still stops without synthesizing those observations into a plan. This is not an oversight. Synthesis would be a form of transfer. A plan would be a form of delegated authority. The book is not unwilling to make a plan. It is unable, given the boundary it has drawn. The blank is not a failure of synthesis. It is the evidence that synthesis would be false.

The ending reframes what it means to read. Reading is often treated as the intake of a tool, the acquisition of a device that can be used later. This text refuses to be that kind of device. The refusal can feel like a denial of utility. But it is not a denial of understanding. Understanding remains, but it remains unarmed, not converted into a method. The blank is the sign of that unarmed understanding.

The ending also makes visible the implicit contract between author and reader. In many texts, the author promises to shoulder the burden of turning insight into direction. The reader pays attention in exchange for relief. Here that contract is declined. The author will not carry the reader's authority, and the reader will not be relieved of the responsibility that cannot be transferred. The decline is not hostile. It is a clear statement that the usual exchange is not available for this subject.

It is important to distinguish between openness and vagueness. The blank is not vague. It is sharply defined by the boundary it marks. Vagueness is the absence of clarity. The blank is the presence of clarity about what cannot be given. The text is precise about the limits of transfer, and that precision is what creates the unresolved ending. The openness is not in the claim. It is in the reader's position relative to that claim.

Discomfort at the end can resemble failure, as if the book has not delivered what it promised. But what the book promised was a description of a boundary, not a set of outcomes. The discomfort is a sign that the reader expected outcomes. That expectation is understandable. The book does not correct it with a final directive. It leaves the expectation exposed, and leaves the boundary standing.

The blank is not nihilism. It does not suggest that nothing matters, or that decisions are empty. On the contrary, it implies that decisions matter enough to require the right authority. If nothing mattered, transfer would be harmless. The refusal to transfer is meaningful only because what is being refused has weight. The blank protects that weight from being reduced to a general statement.

The form of the chapter participates in the refusal. Short lines, breathing spaces, the repeated stop of
bigskip, all work to prevent the text from turning into a smooth, directive speech. The form does not command. It pauses. It keeps the reader in contact with the boundary instead of carrying the reader through it. Form here is not decoration. It is part of the constraint.

Some readers will still try to extract a final verdict, projecting one onto the emptiness. That projection is understandable. It is how reading often works, filling in what is missing to restore a sense of completion. But in this case, the projection is not an extension of the author's authority. It is the reader's own act, separate from the text. The blank makes that separation visible.

The unresolved ending does not mean the subject is unspeakable. The book has spoken at length. What remains unsaid is not the analysis, but the directive. The analysis can be shared. The directive cannot. That is why the book has words and still stops. It is not the limit of language. It is the limit of delegation.

The blank remains even if the reader returns to the earlier chapters. The earlier pages do not soften the ending. They lead to it. The ending is not an omission that could be repaired by reading more carefully. It is the end that the earlier chapters require. The blank is not a hidden page. It is the final page itself.

There is also a political dimension to the refusal to close. Conclusions often serve to legitimate action, to allow decisions to be taken under the banner of a text's authority. When the text refuses to provide that banner, it refuses to be used as a justification for actions it cannot own. This is not a statement against action. It is a statement about the limits of authorial power, about the difference between describing a boundary and licensing a move. The blank keeps that difference visible.

The emotional texture of the blank is quiet. It is not the panic of confusion, and not the relief of resolution. It is a low, steady tension that comes from recognizing that the book will not decide. That tension is not dramatic, and it is not meant to be resolved. It is the affective shape of the boundary itself, felt as a pause that has no signal to end. The chapter ends in that tension, because that is where it must end.

The ending is not a prompt. It does not ask for an answer. It does not wait for completion. It simply stops, and in stopping, it leaves the reader in the space it has described. The blank is not an invitation. It is a line. It remains a line as the book closes, clear, silent, unresolved.

Even the phrase ñecessary blankčan suggest a style, as if the ending were an aesthetic preference. But the blank is not style. It is the residue of a constraint. If the book were written in another voice, with another rhythm, the blank would still be required, because the requirement is not artistic. It is the unavoidable remainder of an argument that refuses to transfer authority. The austerity is not a pose. It is the condition of staying true to the boundary.

It does not soften with repetition. Each return to the ending meets the same edge. The blank does not become so familiar that it disappears. It remains distinct.

The blank persists even as the chapter ends. It does not collapse into a final sentence. It does not become a maxim. It does not transform into a call. It remains a blank. Not empty, not incomplete, not waiting. Simply there.

Acknowledgments

This work was made possible by systems and tools that allowed the structure to be formalized without interruption.

Where errors remain, they are structural and intentional.

About the Author

The author is the compiler and formalizer of the structural framework presented in this volume.

The work does not represent personal opinion, guidance, or individual judgment. Its purpose is to define a closed system of constraints under which judgment may be recognized or invalidated.

No authority is claimed beyond the internal coherence of the structure itself.

www.ingramcontent.com/pod-product-compliance
Lightning Source LLC
Chambersburg PA
CBHW020532030426
42337CB00013B/812